WORK IN THE AGE OF AI: HISTORICAL INSIGHTS AND FUTURE PATHWAYS

PAINTING A BRIGHTER FUTURE

"Technology is not a monster to be feared, but a tool to be wielded. It is a canvas upon which we paint the future, a mirror reflecting our deepest aspirations and anxieties. Like any brushstroke, it can be used for creation or destruction. The choice, as always, lies with us. Let us not be afraid to embrace the potential of what technology offers, but use it with wisdom, compassion, and an unwavering commitment to the betterment of humanity."

WORK IN THE AGE OF AI: HISTORICAL INSIGHTS AND FUTURE PATHWAYS

Empowering Yourself in the Age of AI

RAJ KUMAR

So, why did I write this book? Well, it's simple...

The future is knocking, and it hums with the quiet whir of artificial intelligence. It's a future brimming with possibilities but also tinged with uncertainty. This book, "Work in the Age of AI," isn't just about technology – it's about empowering you.

We're on the cusp of a new era, where AI is woven into the fabric of our lives. Just like the electricity that revolutionized the 20th century, AI will transform the 21st. But unlike electricity, AI isn't just a force acting upon us, it's a tool with the potential to be wielded by us.

This book is your bridge to that future. It's written not for the tech giants, but for everyone – the student curious about a new career path, the artist wondering how AI can unlock creativity, and the parent navigating a world their children will inherit.

My purpose is to demystify the complex world of AI, to make it accessible and understandable. I want to equip you with the knowledge to not just adapt to this future but to shape it actively. Imagine a future where AI isn't a force to be feared, but a collaborator in healthcare, education, and scientific discovery. Imagine a future where AI augments your talents, not replaces them.

"Work in the Age of AI" isn't just a book, it's an invitation. It's an invitation to be a part of the conversation and to understand the opportunities and challenges that lie ahead. Together, let's navigate this exciting new landscape, ensuring AI becomes a tool that empowers, not isolates. The future is here, and with this book, you're ready to embrace it.

CONTENTS

Introduction

Artificial Intelligence, or AI, is a rapidly growing field that is changing the way we live, work, and interact with technology. Fundamentally, AI is the creation of computer systems that are capable of carrying out activities that would typically require human intellect, such as understanding natural language, identifying objects, and making decisions.

The impact of AI on our world is already significant. AI is enhancing the convenience and ease of our lives in a wide range of ways, from voice assistants like Siri and Alexa to self-driving cars and personalized Netflix suggestions. However, AI is not only about comfort; it has the power to completely transform a range of sectors, from healthcare and education to banking and transportation.

What, therefore, makes AI important? There are several causes. First, AI holds the promise of significantly enhancing our lives by automating repetitive jobs and giving us access to new knowledge and abilities. For example, AI can help doctors diagnose diseases more accurately, forecast weather patterns more precisely, and even help humans find love by pairing us with compatible companions.

Second, AI can stimulate economic growth by raising productivity and creating new jobs. According to PwC research, artificial intelligence (AI) might add $15.7 trillion to the global economy by 2030. There is an amazing possibility here for both businesses and people.

Third, artificial intelligence has the potential to address some of the world's most critical issues, including climate change, poverty, and illness. We can create innovative answers to these issues and improve the world by utilizing the potential of AI.

Naturally, AI comes with challenges and risks, just like other powerful technologies. Job displacement, privacy, security, and the ethical application of AI are all issues that raise questions. It is our responsibility to make sure that AI is created ethically so that it may be used for the benefit of humanity.

Chapter 1
The History of AI

Artificial intelligence (AI) is a field of computer science that focuses on building machines that are capable of learning, solving problems, and making decisions—all functions that would typically require human intelligence. With early concepts about mechanical beings and automatons appearing in myths and traditions, the idea of artificial intelligence has been around for ages. But the field of AI research wasn't established until the middle of the 20th century.

Early Ideas and Precursors

Since ancient times, there have been concepts of artificial intelligence (AI). Early thinkers explored the concept of building machines that could think and reason, and philosophers and scientists have always been attracted to this idea.

In his book "De Anima," the ancient Greek philosopher Aristotle discussed the idea that the human mind is a kind of machine and that it is possible to create machines that can think and reason like humans. This is one of the oldest recorded mentions of the concept of intelligent machines. In this work, Aristotle imagined a world in which machines could carry out activities on their own without assistance from humans.

René Descartes, a French philosopher, talked about the possibility of robots mimicking human behavior in his 17th-century work "Discourse on the Method." Descartes believed that animals were essentially complex machines and that it was possible to create machines that could behave similarly.

Similarly, the German philosopher Gottfried Leibniz explored the idea of a "calculus ratiocinator," or a machine that could perform logical operations, in the late 17th century. Leibniz believed that all reasoning could be reduced to a series of calculations and that it was possible to create a machine that could perform these calculations automatically.

These early concepts served as the basis for the creation of artificial intelligence, but it wasn't until the introduction of electronic computers in the middle of the 20th century that the area started to take shape. With the invention of computers, engineers and scientists were able to build tools that could carry out complex calculations at insane speed, creating new opportunities for the creation of intelligent machines.

In summary, Philosophers and scientists have explored the idea of machines capable of thought and reasoning for centuries. These early ideas laid the groundwork for the development of AI, but it wasn't until the invention of electronic computers in the mid-20th century that the field began to take shape.

The Birth of AI

It is the year 1956. The world is a very different place than it is today. Computers are still in their infancy, and the idea of artificial intelligence is still just a dream.

But some scientists and engineers at Dartmouth College are going to revolutionize all of that. They've come together for a summer workshop to talk about artificial intelligence, a brand-new and ambitious area of study.

The scientists at Dartmouth are among the most intelligent people on the planet. They consist of Claude Shannon, Marvin Minsky, and John McCarthy. They are all confident that artificial intelligence (AI) is the future of computing.

The Dartmouth scientists worked on several AI-related projects throughout the summer. They create new techniques and algorithms that enable machines to carry out more difficult tasks. They also create new AI programs that can learn and adapt to new situations.

By the end of the summer, the scientists at Dartmouth had made significant progress in AI research. They have laid the foundation for a new field of science that has the potential to change the world.

The scientists at Dartmouth are the pioneers of AI research. They are the ones who made the dream of artificial intelligence a reality. As a result of their work, AI algorithms have been created and are currently employed in a wide range of applications, from self-driving automobiles to medical diagnosis.

However, the story of AI does not end with the Dartmouth researchers. There is still much to learn in the area of artificial intelligence. Numerous other issues also need to be resolved, such as the possibility of AI being utilized improperly.

But the pioneers of AI have given us a gift. They have shown us that it is possible to create machines that can think for themselves. They have opened up a world of possibilities that we could never have imagined before.

The tale of AI's invention is one of potential and hope. It shows the power of the human imagination. It tells the story of the world that is to come.

Important Figures
The Dreamers, the Pioneers, and the Visionaries

There were dreamers in the beginning. It was philosophers and scientists who imagined a world in which machines could think and reason like humans. They were the first to ask, "Is it possible to create artificial intelligence?"

Aristotle, a Greek mathematician and philosopher, was one of the first to imagine AI. Aristotle mentioned in his book De Anima that the human mind is a type of machine and that it is possible to make machines that can think and reason like humans.

Gottfried Leibniz, a German mathematician, was another early AI dreamer. Leibniz felt it was achievable to develop a universal language capable of translating all human thoughts into symbols. He also believed that it was possible to develop machines that could reason and solve issues using this language.

The dreamers were the ones who began the AI debate. They asked enormous questions and imagined a world beyond our current comprehension. However, it was the pioneers who made AI a reality.

Mathematicians, computer scientists, and engineers who committed their lives to inventing computers that could think and reason were the pioneers. They were the first to make significant advances in AI, laying the foundation for the field as we know it today.

Alan Turing, a British mathematician, was one of the most influential AI pioneers. Many acknowledge Alan Turing as the father of AI, and his Turing Test is still used today to assess machine intelligence. Turing also contributed significantly to the advancement of machine learning and artificial neural networks.

John McCarthy, an American computer scientist, was another significant AI pioneer. McCarthy coined the term "artificial intelligence" in 1955, and he was a key organizer of the 1956 Dartmouth Summer Research Project on Artificial Intelligence. This meeting is largely regarded as the start of the modern era of AI research.

AI became a reality thanks to the pioneers. They created the first AI programs, showing that it was possible to make machines that could think and reason. But it was the visionaries who turned AI into a force for good.

Entrepreneurs, scientists, and engineers are the visionaries who are creating the AI-powered robots that are changing our world. They are developing machines capable of driving vehicles, diagnosing diseases, and writing poems. They are also developing machines that can learn and adapt to new environments, which distinguishes them from previous machines.

Demis Hassabis, a British computer scientist, is another significant AI visionary. Hassabis is a co-founder of DeepMind, the company that created AlphaGo software, which defeated a human Go champion in 2016.

The dreamers, the pioneers, and the visionaries are the people who have shaped the history of artificial intelligence. They are the ones who have made AI a reality, and they will shape the future of AI.

But what is AI's future? Only time will be able to answer that. However, one thing is guaranteed: AI is here to stay and will keep changing the world in unexpected ways.

Key Breakthroughs

Over the years, there have been several significant advancements in the field of AI.

In the 1980s, researchers developed expert systems that were able to emulate human decision-making in specific domains such as medicine and finance. These systems were developed using rule-based reasoning, which means that they were programmed with a set of rules that defined how to solve a particular problem. When an expert system is faced with a new problem, it will utilize its rules to draw conclusions from the given data and make recommendations.

MyCIN, one of the most well-known expert systems, was created in the early 1980s to identify and treat blood infections. Over 400 diseases and their symptoms were defined in a set of guidelines that were encoded into MYCIN. MyCIN would use its rules when given a patient's symptoms to determine the most likely disease and suggest a method of treatment.

Expert systems were a breakthrough in AI in the 1980s. Expert systems proved that it was possible to develop computer programs that could make decisions as complex as those made by humans. However, expert systems also had some limitations. They were only able to solve problems in very specific domains, and they required a lot of time and effort to develop.

Expert systems have made a significant contribution to the science of AI, despite their drawbacks. They paved the way for the creation of more and more complicated AI systems, like deep learning and machine learning. Expert systems also demonstrated how AI might be applied to address real-world issues, and they inspired a new generation of AI researchers.

In the years since the 1980s, expert systems have continued to evolve. They are currently used in a larger variety of applications and are stronger and more adaptable than ever before.

Expert systems are just one example of the many breakthroughs that have been made in AI in recent years. As AI continues to develop, we can expect to see even more amazing breakthroughs in the years to come.

Challenges and Setbacks

The development of AI has faced many difficulties throughout its history. There have been periods known as "AI winters" where funding for AI research has been reduced as a result of disappointment with the results. During these periods, Researchers found it difficult to overcome technical difficulties and meet high expectations.

There have also been continuous discussions regarding AI's ethical implications and worries about the possible effects it may have on society. Some people fear that if advanced AI systems were to become super intelligent or have goals that were in opposition to our own, they may constitute a threat to humanity.

Despite these difficulties, researchers are making progress toward creating increasingly complex AI systems.

Conclusion

The history of artificial intelligence is a fascinating story full of twists and turns. Philosophers and scientists explored the idea of AI in its early beginnings, and now it is a rapidly advancing field with enormous potential. As we look towards the future, it will be exciting to see what breakthroughs await us.

Chapter 2
The Current State of AI: Applications and Challenges

Artificial intelligence (AI) is evolving quickly and has the potential to completely transform a variety of aspects of our lives. Numerous fields, including robotics, computer vision, and natural language processing, now employ AI systems. But some issues must be resolved, including bias, safety, and privacy.

In this chapter, we will explore the current state of AI and discuss its potential applications and challenges. Then, we'll talk about some of the most common AI applications in today's world, including robotics, computer vision, and natural language processing. Finally, we'll look at a few issues like bias, safety, and privacy that must be resolved before AI can completely achieve its potential.

The Current State of AI

The current state of AI is a time of great promise and potential. AI systems are being deployed in a wider variety of applications than ever before as they grow in power and capability. Today, AI technologies are used to diagnose illnesses, predict customer behavior, and improve production processes. They are also being used in self-driving cars, facial recognition systems, and virtual assistants.

In recent years, the cost of creating and using AI systems has decreased, making it more accessible and affordable for businesses and organizations of all kinds. In the coming years, AI will probably become even more widely used as a result of this.

This is leading to several benefits, such as:

- Increased efficiency and productivity: AI systems can automate jobs that were previously performed by people, allowing human workers to focus on more creative and strategic work.
- Improved decision-making: AI systems can analyze large amounts of data to identify patterns and trends that humans may miss. This can help businesses make better decisions about everything from product development to marketing campaigns.
- Personalized experiences: AI systems can be used to personalize products, services, and content for each user. This can lead to a more engaging and satisfying experience for users.

The Potential Applications of AI

The world around us is undergoing rapid change due to artificial intelligence (AI). Artificial intelligence is already significantly affecting our lives, from self-driving cars to virtual assistants. But what are the potential applications of AI in the future?

Here are a few of the most exciting potential applications of AI:

1) Healthcare

AI is being used to develop new diagnostic tools and remedies for diseases. One of the most promising applications of AI in healthcare is in the area of cancer diagnosis. Currently, AI algorithms are better than human doctors at spotting cancer cells in images. For example, research in the journal Nature Medicine reported that DeepDetect, an AI system, could identify breast cancer cells with 99% accuracy, as compared to human radiologists with 94% accuracy.

AI is also being used to create brand-new cancer therapies. For example, an organization by the name of Insilico Medicine is utilizing AI to create brand-new cancer treatments that are specifically targeted to the genetic abnormalities present in each patient's tumor. Compared to traditional cancer treatments, which commonly concentrate on large groupings of cancer cells, this strategy has the possibility of being significantly more effective.

AI is being used to diagnose and treat diseases other than cancer. For example, AI systems are being used to detect diabetes, Alzheimer's disease, and heart disease. Artificial intelligence is also being used to create new vaccines and treatments for infectious diseases.

Although AI in healthcare is still in its early stages, the advantages are huge. AI can completely change how we detect, treat, and prevent disease.

2) Education

Students are given individualized learning opportunities because of AI. AI is being used to create innovative educational games and models, customize learning experiences for students, and automate administrative tasks.

Personalized learning is one of the most exciting uses of AI in education today. AI tools can be used to monitor student development and modify the curriculum as necessary. Students can now study at their own pace and concentrate on the subjects they need the most help with. Additionally, individualized feedback and suggestions can be given to students using AI-powered personalized learning platforms.

The creation of new educational games and simulations is another area where AI is significantly influencing education. Games that are more dynamic and interesting than regular textbooks can be made using AI. AI-powered games can also be used to teach difficult subjects to students entertainingly and interestingly.

Finally, AI is also being used to automate administrative tasks in education. AI systems can be used to grade papers, answer student questions, and manage student records. This frees up teachers to focus on teaching and providing individualized attention to students.

The use of AI in education is still in its early stages, but the potential benefits are huge. AI can completely change how we teach and learn. AI is probably going to have a big impact on education in the future.

3) Business

In business, AI is being used to automate tasks, improve decision-making, and personalize customer experiences. The topic of automation is one of the most interesting uses of AI in business. A wide range of operations, including customer service, marketing, and manufacturing, can be automated with AI systems. Employees are then able to concentrate on more strategic and innovative tasks.

Making decisions is another area of business where AI is having a significant impact. Huge amounts of data can be analyzed by AI systems to find trends and patterns. Making smarter judgments about everything from product development to pricing to marketing may then be done using this information.

Last but not least, personalizing customer experiences is another use of AI. AI technologies can be used to monitor customer preferences and behavior. Customers can then receive customized recommendations and offers as a result of this information. This can aid companies in retaining and gaining new customers.

Although AI in business is still in its earliest stages, the advantages are huge. AI can completely change how companies run. AI is expected to have a significant impact on business in the years to come.

4) Environment

Artificial intelligence (AI) is being used to develop new environmental protection and pollution-reduction devices. For example, AI systems can be used to track wildlife populations and monitor air quality. The development of new renewable energy sources like solar and wind power also makes use of AI.

Here are some specific examples of how AI is being used to protect the environment:

- Wildlife tracking: AI systems are being used to track the population of endangered species, such as elephants and rhinos. This information can help protect these species from poaching and habitat loss.
- Air quality monitoring: AI systems are being used to monitor air quality in real-time. This information can be used to identify areas with high levels of pollution and take steps to reduce them
- Renewable energy: AI is being used to develop new and more efficient ways to harness renewable energy sources, such as solar and wind power. This can help reduce our reliance on fossil fuels and combat climate change.

Although technology is still in its early phases, artificial intelligence has the potential to improve environmental protection significantly. AI has the potential to aid in environmental preservation and the development of a more sustainable future.

These are only a few of the numerous potential uses for AI. We may expect to see even more innovative and surprising applications as AI develops in the next few years.

The challenges of AI

Now, As we all know, Artificial intelligence (AI) has the potential to revolutionize many aspects of our lives. However, there are also several challenges associated with AI that need to be addressed before it can reach its full potential.

One of the biggest challenges in AI is bias. AI systems are educated on data, and if the data is biased, the AI system will be biased as well. Unfair or discriminatory outcomes may result from this.

Another challenge of AI is safety. AI systems can make mistakes, and these mistakes can have serious consequences. For example, an AI-powered self-driving car that makes a mistake could cause a fatal accident. It is important to develop AI systems that are safe and reliable.

Privacy is also a challenge with AI. AI systems can collect and store a lot of data about people. This data could be used to track people's movements, monitor their activities, and even predict their future behavior. This raises concerns about privacy and surveillance.

Finally, there is the challenge of control. Because AI systems are growing more powerful, it's crucial to make sure that humans are in charge of them. In addition to creating ethical standards for the creation and application of AI, we also need to inform the public about the possible drawbacks and advantages of this technology.

Here are some additional challenges of AI that need to be addressed:

1) Interpretability

It can be challenging to understand how AI systems arrive at decisions. Because of this, it may be challenging to trust AI systems and make sure they are making fair and unbiased decisions.

It can be difficult to understand AI systems for several reasons. One explanation is that they often use complicated algorithms that are difficult for people to understand. Another reason is that AI systems are frequently trained on huge datasets that include a wide variety of factors that can affect the choices they make. Due to this, it may be hard to identify the precise elements that influence a decision.

The lack of interpretability in AI systems can have several negative consequences. For example, it can make it difficult to identify and correct biases in AI systems. It can also make it difficult to explain to users how an AI system arrived at a particular decision. This can lead to users distrusting AI systems and refusing to use them.

The interpretability of AI systems can be improved in several ways. One way is by using simpler, more understandable algorithms. Using methods that can aid in the explanation of AI system decisions is another strategy. For example, certain AI systems may come with "explainability engines" that can provide reports explaining how the system came to a answer.

It is important to address the issue of interpretability in AI systems. By making AI systems more interpretable, we can help build trust in these systems and ensure that they are making fair and unbiased decisions.

It's still early days for the field of interpretability in AI. A growing body of work is being done on this subject nonetheless. We could expect greater advancements in the creation of fair and understandable AI systems as this research goes on.

2) Explainability

Explainability is the ability to understand and explain the decisions made by an AI system. This is important for some reasons, including trust, fairness, and accountability.

Users could not trust an AI system and be hesitant to use it if they were unable to understand how its brain decides what to do. Similar to this, to correct discriminatory or unfair decisions made by AI systems, it is necessary to be able to understand the reasoning behind them. Finally, to prevent mistakes from happening again, it is important to be able to understand how an AI system made a mistake that caused harm.

There are some challenges to achieving explainability in AI. One challenge is that AI systems often use complex algorithms that are difficult for humans to understand. Another challenge is that AI systems are often trained on large amounts of data, which can make it difficult to identify the specific factors that influence a decision.

Despite these difficulties, a variety of methods can be applied to increase the clarity of AI systems. Using white-box methods, which require an understanding of the workings of the AI system, is one method. Black-box methods, which focus on giving explanations of the AI system's decisions in terms of the input data and the output outcomes, are another technique.

The best approach to achieving explainability in AI will depend on the specific application. For some applications, white-box methods may be the best option. For other applications, black-box or hybrid methods may be more appropriate.

Explainability is an important area of research in AI. As AI systems get more complicated and powerful, the ability to understand and explain their judgments becomes more important.

3) Alignment

Making sure AI systems are in line with human values is important. This means that AI systems should be designed to function in ways that are helpful to people rather than negative.

There are several challenges to alignment in AI. One challenge is that AI systems are becoming increasingly complex and powerful. This makes it difficult to predict how they will behave in the future. Another challenge is that AI systems are often trained on large datasets that contain a variety of biases. This can lead to AI systems making decisions that are harmful to people.

The issues with alignment in AI can be solved in a variety of ways. Using methods that may help in the detection and correction of biases in AI systems is one strategy. Another strategy is to create AI systems that are clearer and easier to understand. This will make it simpler for people to understand how AI systems function and see potential issues.

It is important to address the issue of alignment in AI. By making sure that AI systems are aligned with human values, we can help ensure that these systems are used for good rather than harm.

AI alignment is a difficult and complex subject, but it is an essential one. We can ensure that AI technologies are used for benefit rather than harm by addressing alignment challenges.

4) Safety

It is essential to make sure AI systems are secure to use. This means that AI systems need to be developed to prevent mistakes that might endanger people or damage property.

These are just some of the challenges of AI. It is important to be aware of these challenges and work to address them. With careful planning and responsible development, AI can be a force for good in the world.

Conclusion

The current state of AI is exciting and promising. AI systems are being deployed in a wider variety of applications than ever before as they grow in strength and capability. However, there are a lot of issues with AI as well, including bias, safety, and privacy. It is essential to be aware of these difficulties and make an effort to overcome them. AI has the potential to be a positive influence in the world with careful planning and responsible development.

chapter 3
The Future of AI: Opportunities and Risks

Imagine a future where AI helps us diagnose diseases, personalize education, optimize resource management and transportation systems, and even automate repetitive tasks in our workplaces. AI's potential to revolutionize our world is immense.

However, along with these exciting possibilities come potential risks. AI could displace workers, lead to biased decisions, raise questions about privacy and human dignity, and even pose security threats.

In this chapter, we will explore the future of AI and its potential implications for humanity. We will talk about the possible advantages and disadvantages of AI as well as how we can make sure that it is used for good rather than bad.

The Potential Benefits of AI

It is the year 2042. The world has changed significantly since a few decades ago. Artificial intelligence (AI) has become a ubiquitous part of our lives, and it is used to solve some of the world's most pressing problems.

The realm of healthcare is one of the most significant areas where AI is used. Medical equipment using AI-powered diagnostics may now identify diseases earlier and more precisely than ever before. For example, AI-powered mammograms can diagnose breast cancer more accurately than human radiologists. AI-powered drug discovery platforms can identify new possible cures for previously thought-to-be incurable diseases.

AI is also being used to improve education. AI-powered tutors can provide personalized learning experiences for students tailored to their individual needs. These instructors are capable of answering questions, providing feedback, and even developing personalized learning plans. Artificial intelligence is also being used to create new instructional tools like augmented reality and virtual reality. These tools can help students learn in new and innovative ways and increase immersion and engagement in the classroom.

In addition to healthcare and education, AI is also being used to solve some of the world's most pressing environmental problems. For example, AI-powered systems are being used to develop more efficient ways to generate and use energy. AI is also being used to develop new technologies to combat climate change.

AI is also being used to improve the lives of people in developing countries. For instance, AI-driven agriculture technologies are being developed to boost crop yields and enhance food security. AI-driven water and sanitation technologies are also being developed to improve water and sanitation services in developing countries.

To be sure, some issues come with the development and application of AI. One of the biggest issues is fear. Some people fear that AI will eventually become so smart that it will dominate the world. Another issue is misuse. AI can be used for malicious purposes, such as weaponization or disinformation.

The good news, though, is that AI has a ton of potential for great things. With a bit of planning and careful development, AI can help make the world even better for everyone.

A group of people who are working to use AI for good:

AI for Good is a non-profit organization of researchers, technologists, and entrepreneurs who are dedicated to harnessing the power of AI to solve the world's most pressing issues. The Foundation's work includes:

- Developing an AI-powered system to predict natural disasters.

- Developing an AI-powered tutor that can provide personalized learning experiences for students.
- Developing AI-powered technologies to combat climate change.
- Developing AI-powered agricultural technologies to increase crop yields and improve food security.

The Foundation's work is not without challenges. There is the fear of AI, the misuse of AI, and the ethical challenges of AI. However, the Foundation is committed to working through these challenges and using AI for good.

AI for Disaster Relief is one of the Foundation's projects. This project aims to create an artificial intelligence (AI)-driven disaster prevention system. The system will be able to predict natural disasters like floods, earthquakes, and hurricanes by analyzing satellite and other data. The system will then be able to alert people in these disaster-prone areas so that they can take preventative measures.

The AI for Good Foundation isn't the only organization working to make the world a better place with AI. As AI advances, we'll see even more incredible outcomes in the years ahead.

The story of the AI for Good Foundation is a story of hope. It is a story about how technology can be used to make the world a better place. It is a story about the power of human ingenuity and compassion. It is a story about the future, and it is a story that we can all be a part of.

The Risks of Artificial Intelligence

AI is a cutting-edge technology that has the potential to change the way we live our lives. But it also comes with some risks, so it's important to be aware of them.

In this section, we'll talk about some of the potential downsides of AI, like job loss, privacy issues, discrimination, and security concerns. We'll also look at ways to help reduce these risks.

1) Job Loss

AI is one of the fastest-evolving technologies in the world. AI's ability to automate many jobs that are currently performed by people is one of its biggest implications. This has raised questions about the future of jobs.

According to a recent McKinsey Global Institute report, the number of jobs that could be lost due to automation is estimated to be 800 million by 2030.

On the other hand, according to the McKinsey Global Institute, the number of new jobs created by AI is estimated to be 900 million.

So, what jobs are most affected by AI? Here are some industries and jobs that are most affected:

- Manufacturing: AI-powered robots are already being used in factories to perform tasks such as welding, painting, and assembly.
- Transportation: Self-driving vehicles and trucks are being developed, which could eventually replace truck drivers, taxi drivers, and other transportation workers.
- Customer service: Chatbots and other AI-powered customer service systems are becoming increasingly sophisticated, and they could eventually replace many human customer service representatives.
- Data entry: AI-powered software is already being used to automate data entry tasks, and this trend is likely to continue.
- Clerical work: AI-powered software can now automate many clerical tasks, such as scheduling appointments, processing invoices, and managing inventory.

Of course, not all jobs are created equal. Jobs that are creative, problem-oriented, and require a high level of social intelligence might be at lower risk of automation. Here are some examples:

- Healthcare: Artificial intelligence is being used to create new medical therapies and diagnostics, but it won't replace doctors and nurses shortly.

- Education: Artificial intelligence can be utilized to deliver personalized learning experiences; however, it is not likely to take the place of teachers.
- Law: AI is being used to automate legal research and drafting, but it is unlikely to replace lawyers.
- Engineering: AI can be used to design and test products, but it is unlikely to replace engineers.

There's no one-size-fits-all answer to the question, "What's the impact of artificial intelligence (AI) on employment?" But there's no denying that AI is changing the way we work. Here's what you need to know.

Here are some ways to mitigate the risks of job loss due to AI:

- Upskill and reskill: Workers need to be prepared to learn new skills to stay ahead of the curve.
- Invest in education: Governments and businesses need to invest in education and training programs to help workers develop the skills they need for the future.
- Create new jobs: Artificial intelligence is also creating new types of jobs, so it's important to create an ecosystem where those jobs can flourish.

It's hard to predict what the future of work will look like, but there's no doubt that artificial intelligence (AI) is going to be a big part of it. Understanding the risks and benefits of AI can help us prepare for what's to come and make sure everyone can benefit from it.

2) **Privacy Violations**

AI is changing the way we live and, with it, our privacy. AI systems are increasingly being used to collect, store, and analyze personal data. This data can be used to track our movements, monitor our online activity, and even predict our behavior.

The potential for privacy violations due to AI is significant. Here are some of how AI can be used to violate privacy:

- Data collection and storage: Artificial intelligence (AI) systems often rely on massive amounts of personal information to train their systems. This information can include your name, address, phone number, email address, financial details, and even your fingerprints or facial scans. And once it's collected, it can be stored indefinitely, even after you forget about it.
- Data analysis: Artificial intelligence systems can analyze our personal information in ways we can't even imagine. They can track our movement, track our online behavior, and even anticipate our behavior. They can use this information to target you with ads, discriminate against you, or even hurt you.
- Data breaches: AI systems can be hacked, just like other computers. If there's a data breach, hackers can get their hands on our personal information and use it for whatever they want.
- Misuse of AI: Governments, businesses, and individuals can misuse AI systems to violate our privacy.

Raj and the AI-Powered Ad

Raj was browsing the web when he came across an advertisement for a new shoe. He was in the mood to buy new shoes. He clicked on the ad, and it took him to a page where he could get more information about the shoe. The page also asked him to provide some personal details like his name, email, and shipping address.

Raj didn't want to give his details, but he did. He thought that the company would only use his details to send him news about the shoes.

A couple of days later, Raj got an email from the company saying that he was eligible for a discount on these shoes. Raj was thrilled and immediately clicked on the e-mail link to buy the shoes.

However, when Raj clicked on that link, it took him to a site he had never visited before. The site then asked him to provide additional personal information, including his credit card and Social Security numbers. Since Raj was suspicious, he chose not to give out his personal information.

Raj later found out that the ad he clicked on was, in fact, an AI-generated ad. The AI used his data to target him with the ad. Similarly, the AI used his data to create a false website that masquerades as the website of the brand that sells the shoes.

Raj's story is a warning sign about what AI can do to our privacy. AI can gather, store, and look at our personal information in ways we can't even imagine.

Here are some points to take away from Raj's story:

- AI systems can be used to collect and store personal data without our knowledge or consent.
- AI systems can be used to target us with advertising that is tailored to our interests and activities.
- AI systems can be used to harm us by hacking into our accounts or by creating fake websites that look like legitimate websites.

But the good news is that there are ways to protect our privacy from AI. Here are some tips:

- Be aware of the risks: One of the first things you need to do to protect your privacy is to understand the risks associated with AI. You need to know how your personal information is being captured, stored, and utilized by AI systems.
- Give consent thoughtfully: If someone asks us to give them permission to collect or use our personal information, we should read the fine print

- Use privacy-friendly settings: Many AI systems have privacy settings that we can use to control how our data is collected and used. We should take the time to configure these settings to our liking.
- Use encryption: Encryption can help to protect our data from being intercepted by hackers. We should use encryption whenever possible, such as sending sensitive information over email or storing it in the cloud.
- Be careful what you share online: The data we share on the internet can be used to monitor us and create a profile of who we are and what we do. We should be mindful of what we post online, especially on social media.

AI is here to stay, but there are some things we can do to keep our personal information safe from it. We should be aware of the potential risks, give our consent carefully, use privacy settings, and encrypt our data.

3) **AI Bias: A Growing Problem**

AI is one of the fastest-evolving technologies in the world. From powering smartphones to making medical decisions, artificial intelligence is changing how we live. But one of AI's biggest challenges is bias.

Before starting we need to know what bias is. So, bias refers to the preferential treatment of one subject over another, often without any objective justification. It can stem from personal experience, opinion, or prejudice.

AI bias occurs when an AI system produces results that are systematically biased against certain groups of people. This can happen in a variety of ways, including:

- The training data is biased: AI systems are made up of data, and if the data is biased, then the AI system will be biased too. For example, an AI facial recognition system that is trained on a dataset of mostly white faces may be more likely to misidentify people of color.
- The AI system is not properly designed: Even if the training data is not biased, the AI system itself can be designed in a way that introduces

bias. For example, an AI system that is designed to predict whether someone is likely to commit a crime may be biased against people of color if it does not properly take other factors into account, such as socioeconomic status.

- The AI system is not used legally: Even if an AI system is not biased itself, it can be used in a biased way. For example, an AI system that is used to make hiring decisions may be biased against women if it is only given access to resumes from men.

AI bias can have several negative consequences, including:

- Discrimination: AI bias can lead to discrimination against certain groups of people. For example, an AI system that is used to make lending decisions may be biased against people of color, resulting in them being denied loans more often than white people.
- Inaccuracy: AI bias can also lead to inaccurate results. For example, a medical AI system that is biased against women may misdiagnose them more often than men.
- Loss of trust: If people believe that AI systems are biased, they may lose trust in these systems and refuse to use them. This can harm the adoption of AI technology.

Several steps can be taken to reduce AI bias, such as:

- Using unbiased training data: This is the most important step in preventing AI bias. The training data should be representative of the population that the AI system will be used.
- Designing AI systems in a fair way: Artificial intelligence systems should consider all relevant factors and not discriminate against any group of people.
- Fairly using AI systems: AI systems should not be used in a way that discriminates against certain groups of people.

AI bias is a complex problem, but it must be addressed if we want to ensure that AI is used for good. By taking steps to prevent AI bias, we can help to create a more fair and equitable world.

4) Security Risks

AI is rapidly changing the way we live and work. From healthcare to transportation to financial services, AI is everywhere. But as AI advances, so do its security risks.

Here are some of the key security risks posed by AI:

- Data poisoning: This is an attack in which malicious data enters an artificial intelligence system to cause it to make inaccurate or malicious decisions.
- Adversarial attacks: These are attacks that take advantage of weaknesses in AI systems to deceive them into making bad decisions. For instance, an attacker could make a deep fake video that appears to be real but is fake. This fake video could be used to trick an artificial intelligence system into making a bad decision that harms the user.
- Model theft: This is the theft of AI models or datasets. This could allow attackers to create their own AI systems that are capable of making the same decisions as the original system. This could be used to commit fraud, spread misinformation, or launch cyberattacks.
- Loss of control: As AI systems become more autonomous, there is a risk that we will lose control over them. This could lead to situations where AI systems make decisions that are harmful to humans. For example, an AI-controlled self-driving car could make a mistake that results in a fatal accident.

These are just a few of the security threats that AI can pose. It's important to understand these threats to reduce them. Here are a few ways to reduce the risks associated with AI:

- Using secure data practices to protect AI training data and models.
- Developing AI systems that are resistant to adversarial attacks.

- Implementing security controls to protect AI systems from being hacked or stolen.
- Addressing AI bias in training data and models.
- Developing ethical guidelines for the development and use of AI.

These are just a few of the dangers associated with AI. Knowing these risks and mitigating them is the best way to ensure that AI is harnessed for good.

Minimizing the Risks of AI

Artificial intelligence (AI) is one of the most transformative technologies of our time. It has the potential to revolutionize many industries and improve our lives in countless ways. However, AI also poses several risks, including bias, safety, security, and privacy.

It is important to take steps to minimize the risks of AI so that we can reap its benefits while safeguarding ourselves from harm. Here are some things we can do:

- Develop ethical guidelines for AI: We need to create clear ethical standards for AI development and use. These standards should cover topics like bias, safety and security, and privacy.
- Invest in AI safety research: We need to invest more research into AI safety. This research should focus on developing methods to make AI systems more reliable, robust, and transparent.
- Regulate AI: We need to create rules and regulations for the development and utilization of artificial intelligence. These rules and regulations should guarantee the safety and ethical use of artificial intelligence systems.
- Educate the public about AI: We need to make sure people know about the risks and advantages of AI. That way, people can make smart choices about how to use it, and AI developers and users can be held accountable.

In addition to the general steps mentioned above, there are a few things you can do to reduce the risk of AI in different situations. For instance, if you're making autonomous vehicles, you can create safety standards for them and make sure they're tested before they're put on the roads. If you're using facial recognition software, you can create policies and procedures to make sure it's used fairly and ethically.

Conclusion

There are indeed risks associated with AI, but they don't have to be the end-all and be-all. Knowing about them and doing what we can to reduce them can help make sure we're using AI for the right reasons and not for the wrong ones.

Chapter 4
AI and Society: Ethical, Legal, and Social Implications

Artificial intelligence (AI) is rapidly transforming our world. From facial recognition software to self-driving cars, AI systems are increasingly making decisions that impact our lives. While AI holds immense potential to improve efficiency, healthcare, and scientific discovery, its development and use raise critical questions about its ethical, legal, and social implications.

This chapter delves into these crucial considerations. We will explore how AI algorithms can perpetuate biases, highlight the challenges of ensuring transparency and explainability in AI decision-making, and discuss the potential privacy concerns associated with data-hungry AI systems.

Furthermore, we will examine the legal complexities surrounding AI, including issues of liability and responsibility for AI actions. We will explore how existing legal frameworks might need to adapt to address algorithmic bias and the ownership of AI and the data that powers it.

The social implications of AI are equally significant. We will discuss the potential for AI to displace jobs through automation, exacerbate social inequalities, and reshape the future of work.

Throughout this chapter, we will emphasize the importance of developing and deploying AI responsibly. We will explore ways to mitigate the risks and ensure that AI benefits all of society.

Ethical Implications of AI

The immense potential of AI comes intertwined with a set of ethical considerations that demand careful attention. Here, we will explore three key areas of ethical concern: bias and fairness, transparency and explainability, and privacy.

1) Bias and Fairness

AI systems are not immune to bias. They can inherit and amplify biases present in the data they are trained on. For instance, an AI algorithm trained on loan applications from a biased historical dataset might perpetuate discrimination against certain demographics when evaluating future applications. These biases can have serious consequences, denying individuals opportunities or unfairly impacting their lives.

To mitigate bias, developers can employ various strategies. One approach is using diverse datasets that represent the population the AI system will interact with. Another method involves fairness audits, which involve testing AI systems for potential bias and identifying areas for improvement.

2) Transparency and Explainability

Many AI systems, particularly complex ones, function as "black boxes." It can be difficult to understand how they arrive at their decisions. This lack of transparency can be problematic. If we don't understand how an AI system makes a decision, it's hard to hold it accountable or trust its judgment in critical situations.

To address this challenge, there's a growing movement towards developing "explainable AI" systems. These systems are designed to provide transparency in their decision-making processes. By offering insights into the reasoning behind an AI's conclusions, explainable AI helps build trust and ensure accountability in AI applications.

3) **Privacy Concerns**

Training powerful AI systems often requires vast amounts of data. This raises privacy concerns, as the data used to train AI systems can be highly personal. There's a risk of data collection practices becoming intrusive, or personal information being misused.

Protecting privacy in the age of AI requires a multifaceted approach. Data anonymization techniques can help mitigate risks. Additionally, robust regulations are needed to ensure responsible data collection practices and safeguard individual privacy.

By addressing these ethical concerns, we can work towards developing and deploying AI in a way that is fair, transparent, and respectful of individual privacy.

Legal Implications of AI

The rapid integration of AI into various aspects of our lives necessitates the development of a robust legal framework to address the complexities and challenges that arise. Here, we will delve into three key areas of legal implication: liability and responsibility, algorithmic bias and legal frameworks, and ownership and intellectual property.

1) **Liability and Responsibility**

One of the most pressing legal questions surrounding AI is: who is responsible for the actions of AI systems? If an AI-powered car malfunctions and causes an accident, who is liable – the manufacturer, the programmer, or the individual using the car?

Determining liability in the context of AI requires clear legal frameworks. Current legal systems may not be well-equipped to handle situations where complex algorithms play a significant role. New legislation might be needed to establish clear lines of responsibility and accountability for the actions and decisions of AI systems.

2) Algorithmic Bias and Legal Frameworks

As discussed earlier, AI algorithms can perpetuate biases present in their training data. This raises legal concerns particularly when AI is used in areas with significant legal ramifications, such as recruitment, loan approvals, or criminal justice.

Existing legal frameworks might not adequately address algorithmic bias. For instance, an AI system used in criminal risk assessment could disproportionately target certain demographics, leading to unequal application of the law. The legal system needs to adapt to ensure fairness and prevent discrimination against individuals based on biased AI decisions. This could involve developing regulations for bias detection and mitigation in AI development, as well as legal recourse for individuals harmed by biased AI systems.

3) Ownership and Intellectual Property

The development and use of AI raise questions regarding ownership. Who owns the data used to train an AI system? Who holds the intellectual property rights to the AI itself? These questions can be particularly complex when multiple parties contribute to the development and training of an AI system.

Clear legal frameworks on ownership are crucial to encourage innovation in AI while protecting the rights of developers and investors. Additionally, intellectual property considerations become relevant when AI systems generate creative outputs, such as music or artwork. The legal system needs to evolve to address these novel challenges presented by AI.

The Social Implications of AI

The social implications of AI are far-reaching and hold the potential to reshape our society in profound ways. Here, we will explore three key areas of social impact: job displacement and automation, socioeconomic inequality, and the future of work and skills.

1) Job Displacement and Automation

One of the most significant concerns surrounding AI is its potential to automate tasks currently performed by humans. AI-powered machines are already replacing workers in various industries, from manufacturing to transportation. While automation can boost efficiency and productivity, it also raises concerns about large-scale job displacement.

The impact of AI on employment will likely vary across sectors. Jobs involving repetitive tasks are more susceptible to automation. However, AI is unlikely to completely replace human workers in the foreseeable future. Many jobs will require a combination of human skills like creativity, critical thinking, and social intelligence, which AI currently struggles to replicate.

To mitigate potential job losses, proactive strategies are necessary. Governments and educational institutions can play a crucial role in retraining and upskilling the workforce to prepare them for the jobs of tomorrow. This may involve encouraging lifelong learning and developing programs that equip individuals with the skills needed to thrive in an AI-driven economy.

2) Socioeconomic Inequality

The rise of AI could exacerbate existing social and economic inequalities. Jobs lost due to automation might disproportionately impact low-skilled workers, potentially widening the income gap. Furthermore, unequal access to the benefits of AI could further disadvantage certain segments of society.

To ensure equitable access to the opportunities presented by AI, investments in education and training are crucial. We need to bridge the digital divide and equip everyone with the necessary skills to participate in the AI revolution. Additionally, policies might be needed to address the potential negative impacts of AI on vulnerable populations.

3) The Future of Work and Skills

AI will undoubtedly transform the nature of work. New jobs will emerge, requiring a different skill set than those currently in demand. The ability to work alongside AI and adapting to a changing work environment will be critical.

Educational systems need to evolve to prepare students for the jobs of the future. Emphasis should be placed on critical thinking, problem-solving, creativity, and collaboration skills. Additionally, lifelong learning will become increasingly important, as individuals will need to continuously update their skills to remain competitive in the workforce.

By acknowledging these social implications and fostering open dialogue, we can work towards developing and deploying AI in a way that benefits all of society. The goal is to harness the power of AI to create a more prosperous, equitable, and fulfilling future for everyone.

The Road Ahead: Towards Responsible AI

The immense potential of AI comes with the crucial responsibility to ensure its development and use are ethical, beneficial, and aligned with human values. This requires a concerted effort from various stakeholders, including:

- Developers and Tech Companies: AI developers should prioritize building fair, transparent, and accountable AI systems. This involves employing diverse teams, implementing robust bias detection methods, and developing user-friendly interfaces that explain how AI decisions are made.
- Governments and Policymakers: Governments have a crucial role to play in establishing regulatory frameworks that promote responsible AI development and deployment. These frameworks could address issues like algorithmic bias, data privacy, and liability for AI actions.
- International Collaboration: The global nature of AI development necessitates international collaboration to ensure responsible practices. This could involve sharing best practices, developing global ethical guidelines for AI, and fostering international cooperation on research and development.

- Individuals and Civil Society: Individuals have a voice in shaping the future of AI. By demanding transparency and accountability from developers and policymakers, we can ensure AI is used responsibly and ethically. Public education regarding AI capabilities and limitations is also crucial for fostering informed dialogue and citizen participation.

Several promising initiatives are already underway to promote responsible AI. For instance, the Partnership on AI is a global effort bringing together leading technology companies, research institutions, and civil society organizations to address the ethical challenges of AI. Additionally, the European Union has taken a proactive stance on AI regulation, proposing legislation that aims to ensure AI systems are safe, trustworthy, and respect fundamental rights.

Looking ahead, continued research and development are crucial for advancing responsible AI. Here are some key areas of focus:

- Developing explainable AI systems: Making AI's decision-making processes more transparent is essential for building trust and ensuring accountability.
- Mitigating algorithmic bias: Ongoing research efforts are needed to develop robust methods for detecting and mitigating bias in AI algorithms and datasets.
- Establishing ethical guidelines for AI development: Developing clear ethical principles and best practices for the creation and use of AI systems will be crucial for responsible development and deployment.

By working together, all stakeholders can navigate the road towards responsible AI. This collaborative effort is essential for ensuring that AI serves humanity and contributes to a more just, equitable, and prosperous future for all.

Conclusion

Ultimately, the path toward responsible AI demands a collaborative effort. Developers, policymakers, international organizations, and individuals all have a role to play. By fostering open dialogue, prioritizing ethical considerations, and continuously working towards responsible development and deployment, we can ensure AI benefits society as a whole. The future of AI is not predetermined. Through informed choices and collaborative action, we can shape an AI-driven future that is equitable, sustainable, and empowers humanity to flourish.

chapter 5
AI and Work: How AI is Transforming Industries and Jobs

The emergence of artificial intelligence (AI) can be considered one of the most important technological breakthroughs in recent history. Its influence goes well beyond the boundaries of science fiction, deeply changing our lifestyles, work environments, and interactions with our surroundings. This effect is particularly noticeable in the professional sector. AI is swiftly changing various sectors, streamlining activities, and changing the fundamental aspects of employment. This section explores the complex bond between AI and employment, examining its transformative possibilities, the obstacles it brings, and the competencies essential for success in an era driven by AI.

The Automation Revolution

One of the most visible impacts of AI is automation. AI-powered systems can handle a wide range of tasks with unmatched speed, accuracy, and efficiency. These tasks include data entry, customer service inquiries, quality control in manufacturing, and even aspects of financial trading and legal research.

The automation revolution has undoubtedly led to concerns about job displacement. Repetitive, rule-based jobs are most susceptible to being replaced by AI. Sectors like manufacturing, transportation, and administrative services are likely to experience significant automation. A 2017 study by McKinsey Global Institute estimated that between 73 million and 375 million jobs could be displaced worldwide by automation by 2030.

However, the narrative of AI as a "job-killer" is not entirely accurate. Automation also creates new opportunities. New jobs emerge in the design, development, deployment, and maintenance of AI systems. Data scientists, machine learning engineers, robot programmers, and AI ethicists are just some examples of these new roles.

The impact of automation is likely to be uneven across industries and skill levels. While some jobs disappear, others will be created, but the skillsets required will be vastly different. The key lies in understanding the nature of automation and how it interacts with human capabilities.

Beyond Automation: AI as a Collaborator

AI excels at handling vast amounts of data and identifying patterns. This frees up human workers to focus on tasks that require uniquely human skills – creativity, critical thinking, emotional intelligence, and social skills. AI is increasingly seen as a collaborator, augmenting human capabilities rather than replacing them.

Consider the healthcare industry. AI can analyze medical scans with incredible accuracy, highlighting potential abnormalities. This allows doctors to focus on diagnosis, treatment planning, and patient interaction, areas where empathy, communication, and critical thinking are paramount. Similarly, in customer service, AI-powered chatbots can handle routine inquiries, freeing up human agents to address complex issues requiring empathy and problem-solving skills.

This collaborative approach extends beyond specific tasks. AI can augment human decision-making by providing real-time data analysis and insights. For instance, in finance, AI algorithms can analyze market trends and identify potential risks, allowing financial analysts to make more informed investment decisions.

The rise of AI necessitates a shift in how we view the future of work. We are moving towards a more collaborative model where humans and machines work together, leveraging their respective strengths to achieve optimal results.

The Rise of New Jobs and the Reskilling Imperative

The AI revolution will undoubtedly create new job opportunities, but these jobs will require a different skill set than traditional jobs. Here's a breakdown of some emerging job categories:

- AI Development and Engineering: Data scientists, machine learning engineers, robot programmers, and AI ethicists will be crucial for designing, developing, deploying, and maintaining AI systems.
- Human-Machine Collaboration: These roles will involve facilitating seamless interaction and collaboration between humans and AI systems. This might involve developing user interfaces, training algorithms, and ensuring effective communication.
- Data Management and Analysis: The ability to collect, analyze, and interpret vast amounts of data will be crucial across industries. Data analysts, data visualization specialists, and business intelligence professionals will be in high demand.
- Cybersecurity: As reliance on AI grows, so do cybersecurity threats. Cybersecurity specialists with expertise in protecting AI systems and data will be essential.

The key to navigating this job landscape lies in reskilling and upskilling the existing workforce. Educational institutions and training programs need to adapt to equip individuals with the skills needed to thrive in the AI-powered workplace. This includes:

- Technical Skills: Programming languages like Python and R, data analysis skills, and a basic understanding of AI concepts.
- Soft Skills: Critical thinking, problem-solving, creativity, communication, and collaboration skills will be essential for working alongside AI systems.

- Adaptability and Lifelong Learning: The ability to learn new skills and adapt to changing technologies will be crucial for long-term career success.

Governments, educational institutions, and businesses all have a role to play in facilitating reskilling initiatives and ensuring a smooth transition to the AI-powered future of work.

Conclusion

AI is not a job-killing machine, but rather a transformative force that will reshape the future of work. By embracing lifelong learning, developing essential skills, and advocating for responsible AI development, we can ensure that AI works for us, not against us. The future workplace presents both challenges and opportunities. By taking a proactive approach and fostering a human-centered approach to AI, we can create a future where AI empowers workers, enhances productivity, and fosters a more equitable and prosperous world.

Chapter 6
AI and Education: How AI is Enhancing Learning and Teaching

Imagine a classroom where each student receives a personalized learning experience, one that caters to their unique strengths, weaknesses, and learning pace. This isn't science fiction; it's the promise of Artificial Intelligence (AI) in education. Traditionally, education has relied on a one-size-fits-all approach, leaving many students feeling disengaged or overwhelmed. AI, however, offers a paradigm shift. By leveraging intelligent algorithms and data analysis, AI can transform education into a dynamic and personalized journey, fostering a deeper love of learning for all. This chapter delves into the exciting possibilities of AI in education, exploring how it can unlock student potential, empower educators, and ultimately shape the future of learning.

The Potential of AI in Education

The educational landscape is undergoing a significant transformation driven by the rise of Artificial Intelligence (AI). No longer confined to the realm of science fiction, AI is rapidly making its way into classrooms, offering a plethora of opportunities to personalize learning, enhance skill development, improve accessibility, and increase efficiency.

1) **Personalized Learning: Tailoring Education to Individual Needs**

One of the most significant promises of AI in education lies in its ability to personalize learning experiences. Traditional education often employs a one-size-fits-all approach, neglecting the unique learning styles and paces of individual students. AI, however, can revolutionize this by utilizing sophisticated algorithms to assess student strengths, weaknesses, and learning preferences. This data can then be used to curate personalized learning plans, delivering content, exercises, and feedback tailored to each student's specific needs.

Imagine a student struggling with fractions. An AI-powered platform could identify this difficulty and create a customized learning path. It might present interactive games that make practicing fractions fun, utilize real-world examples to make the concepts more relatable, and offer targeted feedback to bridge any knowledge gaps. This personalized approach fosters a deeper understanding and keeps students engaged, fostering a love for learning that transcends rote memorization.

Adaptive learning platforms are prime examples of AI in action. These platforms leverage AI algorithms to analyze student performance in real time. Based on the results, the platform dynamically adjusts the difficulty level of the content, suggests additional resources, and provides personalized feedback. This continuous adaptation ensures students are constantly challenged and learning within their optimal zone, preventing boredom with repetitive tasks or frustration with insurmountable difficulty.

Furthermore, AI tutors powered by natural language processing (NLP) can create a more interactive and engaging learning environment. These virtual tutors can conversationally answer student questions, provide explanations tailored to individual learning styles, and offer immediate feedback on assignments. This personalized attention can significantly improve learning outcomes, especially for students who may feel hesitant to ask questions in a traditional classroom setting.

2) **Enhanced Skill Development: Beyond Traditional Subjects**

While core academic subjects remain crucial, the future of education emphasizes the development of essential 21st-century skills such as critical thinking, problem-solving, collaboration, and communication. AI can play a vital role in fostering these skills by offering innovative learning experiences.

Gamification, a technique that incorporates game mechanics into learning activities, is a powerful tool for AI. AI-powered educational games can create immersive and engaging environments where students learn while playing. These games can be designed to test and develop critical thinking skills, encourage problem-solving through scenario-based challenges, and promote collaboration through team-based activities. Additionally, AI can analyze gameplay data to identify areas where students might need further support, allowing teachers to intervene and provide targeted guidance.

Furthermore, AI can facilitate simulations that provide students with safe spaces to practice real-world scenarios. Imagine a virtual reality program that allows students to conduct historical simulations, run businesses in a simulated economy, or navigate complex ethical dilemmas. These immersive experiences allow students to learn by doing, fostering critical thinking, decision-making skills, and problem-solving abilities that are crucial for success beyond the classroom.

3) **Improved Accessibility and Support: Breaking Down Barriers to Learning**

The power of AI extends to making education more inclusive and accessible for all students. AI-powered language translation tools can break down language barriers, allowing students from diverse backgrounds to access educational content in their native languages. This fosters a more inclusive learning environment and empowers students to excel without language limitations.

For students with disabilities, AI can be a game-changer. Text-to-speech applications can assist students with visual impairments by reading aloud text from textbooks and other learning materials. AI-powered captioning tools can transcribe lectures for students who are deaf or hard of hearing, ensuring equal access to information. Additionally, AI can be used to create personalized learning plans for students with learning difficulties, providing them with the support and targeted instruction they need to thrive.

4) Increased Efficiency and Scalability: Empowering Educators

The potential of AI in education extends beyond directly impacting students. AI can significantly improve the efficiency of the educational system, freeing up valuable time for teachers. AI-powered tools can automate tedious administrative tasks such as grading essays, multiple-choice tests, and quizzes. This allows teachers to focus their energy on more meaningful interactions with students, such as providing personalized feedback, facilitating discussions, and designing engaging learning activities.

Furthermore, AI can personalize instruction at scale. Imagine a crowded classroom with students at different learning paces. AI can analyze student data and suggest differentiated instruction strategies for the teacher, allowing them to cater to the individual needs of each student despite class size limitations.

Challenges and Considerations of AI in Education

While the potential of AI in education is undeniable, its implementation comes with a set of challenges and considerations that educators and policymakers must carefully navigate. Here, we delve into these complexities, exploring the need for teacher training, addressing algorithmic bias, ensuring data privacy, and charting a course for a responsible and ethical future of AI-powered learning.

1) Teacher Training and Support: Bridging the Gap Between Humans and Machines

The successful integration of AI in classrooms hinges on the preparedness of educators. Traditionally trained teachers may lack the technical expertise and pedagogical skills required to effectively utilize AI tools. To bridge this gap, comprehensive professional development programs must be implemented. These programs should equip teachers with the knowledge to:

- Evaluate and select AI tools: Teachers need to be discerning consumers of AI technologies. Training programs can help them assess the efficacy and alignment of AI tools with their curriculum and learning objectives.
- Integrate AI effectively: Simply incorporating AI tools isn't enough. Training should focus on how to seamlessly integrate AI into existing lesson plans, maximizing their benefits for student learning.
- Utilize AI for data-driven instruction: AI provides teachers with a wealth of student data. Training programs should equip educators with the skills to analyze this data and use it to inform personalized instruction and interventions.

Furthermore, fostering a collaborative environment with AI is crucial. Teachers are not meant to be replaced; they are the human element that guides, inspires, and fosters critical thinking skills in students. Training programs should emphasize the complementary role of AI, empowering teachers to leverage its capabilities to enhance their teaching practices.

2) Algorithmic Bias and Fairness: Mitigating the Risks of Unequal Learning

One of the most pressing concerns regarding AI in education is the potential for algorithmic bias. AI algorithms are only as good as the data they are trained on. If these datasets contain biases, the resulting AI tools will perpetuate those biases in student learning. For example, an AI-powered learning platform trained on biased data might recommend different learning paths for students based on race or gender.

Mitigating algorithmic bias requires a multi-pronged approach. First, educators and developers need to be aware of potential biases within data sets and take steps to diversify them. Additionally, AI algorithms need to be designed with fairness in mind, incorporating mechanisms to detect and correct for bias. Finally, ongoing monitoring and evaluation of AI tools are essential to ensure they are delivering equitable learning experiences for all students.

3) **Data Privacy and Security: Protecting Student Information**

The use of AI in education raises significant concerns regarding data privacy and security. AI platforms collect and analyze a vast amount of student data, including learning progress, test scores, and potentially even facial recognition data. Protecting this sensitive information requires robust safeguards.

Educational institutions need to implement clear data privacy policies outlining how student data is collected, stored, and used. Students and their families should be informed of these policies and have control over their data. Additionally, robust cybersecurity measures are essential to prevent unauthorized access to student data.

A Responsible Future for AI in Education

AI presents a transformative opportunity for education, but its implementation must be approached with caution and a commitment to ethical practices. By addressing the challenges of teacher training, algorithmic bias, and data privacy, we can ensure that AI empowers educators and fosters a learning environment that is personalized, inclusive, and prepares students for the future. Here are some key takeaways for a responsible future of AI in education:

- Human-centered approach: AI should be seen as a tool to enhance the role of teachers, not replace them.
- Focus on equity and fairness: Algorithmic bias must be mitigated to ensure equal learning opportunities for all students.
- Transparency and accountability: Data collection and usage policies should be transparent and accountable to students, parents, and educators.

- Continuous learning and improvement: The development and use of AI in education should be an ongoing process of learning, adapting, and refining to maximize its benefits for learners.

By prioritizing ethics and responsibility, we can harness the power of AI to create a future where education is not just standardized, but truly transformative, empowering each student to thrive.

The Future of AI and Education

The merging of artificial intelligence (AI) with education holds the promise of a vibrant and tailored educational journey that has never been experienced before. Looking ahead, a variety of thrilling opportunities arise, molding the future of educational settings and our approach to learning. Here, we delve into possible future uses of AI, the changing duties of educators, and the significance of working together with machines to achieve the best results in learning.

1) AI-Powered Learning Experiences

One exciting future application of AI lies in immersive learning experiences. Imagine virtual reality (VR) simulations that transport students to the heart of historical events, allowing them to interact with historical figures and environments. AI can personalize these simulations, tailoring the experience to individual learning styles and interests. This fosters a deeper understanding of history and ignites a passion for learning that transcends textbooks and lectures.

Furthermore, AI-powered learning platforms can become even more sophisticated, leveraging big data and advanced analytics to predict student needs and recommend personalized learning pathways. These pathways could incorporate adaptive learning software that adjusts content difficulty based on student performance, curate educational resources tailored to learning styles, and offer targeted interventions for identified knowledge gaps.

2) **AI as a Career Guidance Tool**

The future of AI holds immense potential for personalized career guidance. AI-powered career assessments can delve deeper, analyzing a student's academic performance, personality traits, and skillsets to recommend suitable career paths. These recommendations can be further refined by considering factors like current job market trends and projected future growth in specific industries. This personalized approach empowers students to make informed career decisions, aligning their passions with in-demand skills.

3) **Evolving Role of Teachers**

The rise of AI doesn't signal the end of teachers; instead, it ushers in a new era for their role. With AI handling repetitive tasks like grading and providing basic instruction, teachers can focus on what they do best – fostering critical thinking, creativity, and collaboration skills in students. Teachers will become facilitators who guide students through personalized learning journeys, provide emotional support, and encourage them to become independent learners.

4) **Human-Machine Collaboration**

The future of AI in education isn't about machines replacing teachers; it's about humans and machines working together to create optimal learning environments. AI can automate tasks, personalize learning, and provide data-driven insights, but it cannot replicate the human touch and emotional intelligence essential for effective learning.

Teachers, with their deep understanding of learner psychology and ability to inspire and motivate, remain the cornerstone of education. AI, on the other hand, excels at analyzing data and tailoring learning experiences. This human-machine collaboration leverages the strengths of both, maximizing the potential for student growth and development.

Conclusion

AI presents a transformative vision for the future of education. From personalized learning pathways to immersive learning experiences, AI holds immense potential to empower students and enhance the teaching profession. However, navigating this future requires careful consideration of teacher training, algorithmic fairness, and data privacy. By prioritizing ethical practices and human-machine collaboration, we can unlock the full potential of AI to create a future where education is not just standardized, but truly transformative.

Chapter 7
AI and Health

In the tangled web of human history, healthcare is a place of hope. A place where pain is comforted and life returns to normalcy. But today, this noble realm is about to be transformed in ways we have never seen before. Artificial intelligence (AI) is set to revolutionize the very nature of medical practice.

At the core of AI's innovation is its ability to sift through massive amounts of data, uncovering hidden patterns and insights. This is especially true in medical imaging, where AI can identify subtle anomalies in X-ray, CT, and MRI images, allowing for earlier and more precise diagnoses.

AI's impact extends beyond diagnostics, revolutionizing the field of drug discovery and development. By analyzing vast datasets of molecular and clinical data, AI can identify promising drug candidates, predict their efficacy and potential side effects, and accelerate the process of bringing new treatments to patients.

So, In this chapter, we will explore the fascinating intersection of AI and health, delving into the myriad ways in which this powerful technology is shaping the future of healthcare delivery.

We will examine how AI is revolutionizing diagnosis and treatment, enabling personalized medicine, and accelerating drug discovery. We will also discuss the ethical considerations surrounding the use of AI in healthcare and explore the role of healthcare professionals in the AI-driven future of medicine.

Join us on this exciting journey as we uncover the transformative potential of AI in healthcare.

Firstly let's talk about the present situation of healthcare and wellbeing.

Present Situation of Healthcare and Wellbeing

The current state of healthcare is facing several challenges. These challenges include:

- The rising cost of healthcare: Healthcare is increasing faster than inflation. This is making it difficult for people to afford the care they need.
- The shortage of healthcare workers: There is a shortage of healthcare workers in many parts of the world. This is making it difficult to provide timely and quality care to patients.
- The increasing complexity of diseases: Diseases are becoming more complex, making diagnosing and treating them difficult.
- The lack of access to healthcare: Not everyone has access to quality healthcare. This is especially true in developing countries.

We see some of the problems in healthcare now but in the future, this can be minimized with the help of AI.

Example:

Emily Whitehead and Cancer

In 2017, Emily Whitehead, a 22-year-old woman, received a devastating diagnosis: Stage 4 synovial sarcoma, a rare and aggressive cancer. After undergoing conventional treatments like surgery and chemotherapy, her cancer persisted.

Traditional options seemed exhausted, and Emily's future was uncertain. However, hope emerged with the involvement of the Memorial Sloan Kettering Cancer Center (MSK). MSK's doctors, in collaboration with IBM Research, utilized a powerful AI tool called Watson for Oncology. Watson analyzed Emily's complex medical data, including genetic information, medical history, and treatment responses. By sifting through this vast data, Watson identified a potential treatment option that had never been used for Emily's type of cancer before - a combination of two drugs, pembrolizumab and eribulin.

Initially hesitant, Emily and her doctors decided to give this AI-driven recommendation a chance. And to their surprise, it worked wonders. The combined therapy shrunk Emily's tumor significantly, allowing her to live a relatively cancer-free life since then.

Emily's story exemplifies the remarkable potential of AI in cancer treatment. AI can analyze vast amounts of data with unprecedented speed and accuracy, unearthing hidden patterns and unlocking personalized treatment options that were previously unknown.

So, now let us talk about how AI is improving Healthcare and wellbeing.

Diagnostic Advancements with AI

Imagine a world where your doctor can detect a disease with uncanny accuracy, even before you experience any symptoms. This is not science fiction; it's the reality of diagnostic advancements with artificial intelligence (AI), a technology revolutionizing healthcare as we know it.

From Scans to Predictions: AI's ability to analyze vast amounts of medical data, including images, lab results, and patient records, is leading to unprecedented breakthroughs in diagnostics. Take medical imaging, for example. By meticulously analyzing X-rays, CT scans, and MRIs, AI algorithms can detect subtle abnormalities that the human eye might miss, paving the way for early detection of diseases like cancer, heart disease, and neurological disorders.

However, the impact of AI goes beyond image analysis. AI is also changing the way we view patient data. By recognizing patterns and correlations within large data sets, AI can predict health risks and identify those at high risk of complications. This means doctors can intervene earlier and prevent the development of serious diseases.

The integration of AI into diagnostic workflows is leading to several benefits, including improved diagnostic accuracy, reduced turnaround times, and personalized treatment plans. AI is also helping to democratize healthcare by providing access to advanced diagnostic tools to underserved communities.

As AI technologies keep advancing, we can expect even more innovative applications in diagnostics. AI-powered tools are being developed to analyze real-time patient data, enabling continuous monitoring of patient health and early detection of potential complications.

The advancements in AI-powered diagnostics are changing the healthcare landscape, paving the way for a future where diseases are detected earlier, treated more effectively, and managed more proactively. AI is empowering healthcare providers to deliver personalized, precise, and predictive care, ultimately leading to improved patient outcomes and a healthier population.

Personalized Medicine and Treatment Plans

For centuries, healthcare followed a "one-size-fits-all" approach, where the same treatment was prescribed to all patients diagnosed with the same condition. However, this often led to suboptimal outcomes, with some patients experiencing little to no improvement and others suffering from severe side effects. Thankfully, the rise of personalized medicine is ushering in a new era of customized care, promising improved outcomes and a more patient-centric approach.

What is personalized medicine?

Personalized medicine, also known as precision medicine, tailors healthcare interventions to the unique characteristics of each patient. This involves analyzing a wide range of factors, including:

- Genetics: Genetic analysis can help identify risk factors for certain diseases, anticipate treatment reactions, and detect adverse reactions.
- Biomarkers: These are biological molecules that indicate the presence or progression of a disease. By measuring biomarkers, doctors can personalize drug dosages and monitor treatment effectiveness.

- Genetics: Genetic analysis can help identify risk factors for certain diseases, anticipate treatment reactions, and detect adverse reactions.
- Biomarkers: These are biological molecules that indicate the presence or progression of a disease. By measuring biomarkers, doctors can personalize drug dosages and monitor treatment effectiveness.
- Medical history: A patient's past medical history, including previous diagnoses, treatments, and responses, provides valuable insights for personalized treatment plans.
- Lifestyle factors: Environmental factors, such as diet, exercise, and smoking habits, can significantly impact health. Personalized medicine integrates these factors into treatment plans for optimal results.

The Rise of Personalized Medicine

The rise of personalized medicine is largely driven by advances in genomics and other omics technologies, which enable us to understand the individual's unique biological makeup at a deeper level. This knowledge can be used to predict an individual's risk of developing certain diseases, identify potential drug targets, and develop personalized treatment plans.

Benefits of Personalized Medicine

Personalized medicine offers several potential benefits over traditional one-size-fits-all approaches, including:

- Improved Treatment Efficacy: By tailoring treatments to the individual's unique genetic and biological makeup, personalized medicine can increase the effectiveness of treatment and reduce the risk of side effects.
- Reduced Healthcare Costs: By targeting interventions to those who are most likely to benefit, personalized medicine can help reduce unnecessary testing and treatment, leading to cost savings for both patients and healthcare systems.
- Enhanced Patient Engagement: By involving patients in their own healthcare decisions, personalized medicine can lead to better patient

engagement and adherence to treatment plans.

Challenges and Opportunities

While personalized medicine holds great promise, several challenges need to be addressed for it to reach its full potential. These challenges include:

- Access to data: Collecting and analyzing the large amounts of data required for personalized medicine can be expensive and time-consuming.
- Data privacy: Concerns about data privacy and security need to be addressed to ensure that patients are comfortable sharing their personal information.
- Regulatory hurdles: Regulatory frameworks need to be updated to accommodate the development and use of personalized medicine technologies.
- Cost-effectiveness: Demonstrating the cost-effectiveness of personalized medicine interventions is crucial for its widespread adoption.

Despite these challenges, there is a growing consensus that personalized medicine is the future of healthcare.

The Future of Personalized Medicine

The future of healthcare is undoubtedly personalized. As technology advances and the cost of genetic testing decreases, personalized medicine will become more widely available. We can expect to see:

- Improved diagnostic tools: New technologies like gene expression analysis and proteomics will offer a deeper understanding of individual biology, leading to more accurate diagnoses and personalized treatment plans.

- Development of new drugs and therapies: With a deeper understanding of the genetic basis of diseases, researchers can develop new drugs and therapies tailored to specific patient populations, leading to more effective and personalized treatment options.
- Focus on prevention: With the ability to predict disease risk, personalized medicine will shift the focus towards preventive measures and early intervention strategies, ultimately promoting better overall health and well-being.

Personalized medicine represents a paradigm shift in healthcare, moving away from a one-size-fits-all approach towards a future where treatment plans are designed specifically for each individual. By harnessing the power of genetics and other factors, personalized medicine is promising to improve patient outcomes, reduce healthcare costs, and foster a future of proactive, preventive healthcare.

Predictive Analytics for Disease Prevention

Imagine a world where healthcare isn't just about treating illnesses but preventing them altogether. Predictive analytics, a powerful tool using data science, is making this a reality. Let's explore how it works and how it can benefit you!

What is Predictive Analytics for Disease Prevention?

Predictive analytics for disease prevention is a data-driven approach using advanced statistical models to identify individuals at high risk for developing certain diseases. This approach involves analyzing large amounts of data, including medical records, genetic information, lifestyle factors, and environmental factors, to identify patterns and trends that can predict the likelihood of developing a disease.

The goal of predictive analytics for disease prevention is to identify individuals who are at high risk for developing a disease and intervene early to prevent the onset of the disease. This approach is particularly useful for chronic diseases, such as diabetes, heart disease, and cancer, which are often preventable with early intervention.

How Does it Help Prevent Disease?

Here's the magic:

- Early Detection: Predictive models can analyze your data and flag potential risks for diseases like diabetes or heart disease. This allows doctors to intervene early before symptoms even appear.
- Personalized Prevention: Forget one-size-fits-all approaches. Predictive analytics helps tailor preventive measures to your specific needs. If you're at risk for heart disease, doctors might recommend exercise programs and cholesterol checks.
- Resource Management: Healthcare systems can use predictive analytics to identify high-risk populations and allocate resources more efficiently. Imagine focusing preventive efforts on people who need them most!

Examples in Action:

Disease	How Predictive Analytics Helps
1) Diabetes	A model analyzes your blood sugar, family history, and weight to predict diabetes risk. If it's high, doctors can recommend dietary changes or preventative medications.
2) Heart Disease	By analyzing your blood pressure, cholesterol, and lifestyle, doctors can predict your risk for heart disease. Early intervention with medication or lifestyle changes could prevent a heart attack.
3) Cancer	Genetic testing combined with family history can identify individuals at high risk for certain cancers. Early detection through regular screenings significantly improves treatment outcomes.

Benefits for Everyone:

Predictive analytics is a win-win for both individuals and healthcare systems:

- Individuals: You can take control of your health by understanding your risks and taking preventive measures. Early detection often leads to easier and more successful treatment.
- Healthcare Systems: By focusing on prevention, healthcare systems can reduce the number of people who develop chronic diseases. This translates to lower costs and improved public health outcomes.

The Future is Preventive:

Predictive analytics is still evolving, but its potential is vast. Imagine a future where personalized health plans become the norm, and diseases are prevented before they even start. As data science continues to develop, predictive analytics will play a crucial role in shaping a healthier future for everyone.

Virtual Health Assistants and Telemedicine

Imagine having a healthcare assistant available 24/7, ready to answer questions, schedule appointments, and even offer basic health advice – all from your phone or computer. That's the magic of virtual health assistants (VHAs) working alongside telemedicine!

Telemedicine 101:

Telemedicine simply means using technology to deliver healthcare remotely. Think video calls with doctors, specialists you can consult from anywhere, or even refilling prescriptions online. It's healthcare on the go, making it easier to access medical services, especially for those in remote areas or with busy schedules.

Enter the Virtual Assistant:

VHAs are like digital sidekicks for both patients and healthcare providers in this telemedicine world. They use artificial intelligence (AI) to offer a range of helpful services:

- Scheduling whizzes: VHAs can streamline appointment booking. They can find suitable slots in doctors' calendars, send you reminders, and even handle appointment changes. No more phone tag!
- Information at your fingertips: VHAs can answer basic health questions you might have about symptoms, medications, or general health topics. Think of them as a friendly health information concierge.
- Keeping you on track: Did you forget to take your meds today? A VHA can send gentle reminders to ensure you stay on top of your treatment plan.
- Mental health support: Some VHAs offer basic mental health support through chatbots or guided exercises, helping you manage stress or anxiety.
- Telehealth champions: VHAs can help set up your video call with the doctor, ensuring a smooth telemedicine experience.

Benefits for Everyone:

This dynamic duo of VHAs and telemedicine brings a wave of benefits:

- Convenience: Get the healthcare you need from the comfort of your home. No more waiting rooms!
- Improved access: People in remote areas or with mobility issues can now connect with specialists more easily.
- Better communication: VHAs can translate languages or clarify medical jargon, ensuring clear communication between patients and doctors.
- Preventive care: Easier access to healthcare can encourage regular checkups and preventive measures.

- Reduced costs: Telemedicine appointments can sometimes be more affordable than traditional in-person visits.

Things to Consider:

While VHAs and telemedicine are a powerful combo, there are some things to keep in mind:

- Technology access: Not everyone has access to reliable internet or devices needed for telemedicine.
- Data privacy: Ensuring the security of your medical information is crucial.
- Complex conditions: Not all health concerns are suitable for telemedicine consultations. In-person examinations might still be necessary.

The Future of Virtual Care:

The future of healthcare is looking more virtual, with VHAs likely becoming even more sophisticated. Imagine AI assistants reminding you to get your flu shot or even helping monitor chronic conditions. Telemedicine, powered by VHAs, has the potential to make healthcare more accessible, convenient, and personalized for everyone.

Remember: VHAs and telemedicine are excellent tools, but they shouldn't replace traditional in-person care entirely. It's all about having the right option for your specific needs and working together with your doctor for optimal health.

Drug discovery and development

Drug discovery and development is a complex and time-consuming process that involves identifying and developing new medications to treat diseases and improve human health. It typically takes years and billions of dollars to bring a new drug to market, making it a challenging and costly endeavor for pharmaceutical companies. However, with the advancements in technology, specifically artificial intelligence (AI), drug discovery and development are becoming more efficient and effective. Here, we will explore the role of AI in drug discovery and development and provide insights into how it is expediting the process. We will also discuss some examples of AI algorithms that are accelerating drug development.

Drug Discovery and Development: Harnessing AI for Faster Results

Drug discovery and development is a multi-step process that involves identifying a potential drug target, designing and synthesizing compounds, testing their efficacy and safety, and obtaining regulatory approval. Traditionally, this process has been done manually by scientists, which is not only time-consuming but also prone to human error. However, with the emergence of AI, this process is becoming more efficient and accurate.

AI in Drug Discovery

Artificial intelligence (AI) is a broad term used to describe a wide range of technologies, including machine learning (ML), natural language processing (NLP), and robotics. All of these technologies are capable of analyzing large amounts of information, recognizing patterns, and making predictions, which makes them ideal tools for drug research and development.

One of the most prominent uses of AI in drug discovery has been in the area of virtual screening.

Virtual screening involves the use of computer algorithms to sift through large chemical databases and identify drug candidates. The process is much quicker and more precise than lab-based drug screening, which involves testing each compound individually.

AI is also being used to analyze and interpret data from clinical trials. By analyzing data from previous trials, AI algorithms can identify patterns and predict the success of future trials. This can help pharmaceutical companies make more informed decisions about which drugs to pursue and which ones to discontinue.

AI in Drug Development

Once a potential drug candidate has been identified, the next step is to develop it into a safe and effective medication. This process involves testing the drug in various preclinical and clinical trials, which can take years and cost millions of dollars. However, with the help of AI, this process is becoming more efficient and cost-effective.

Preclinical and clinical trial data can be analyzed by AI algorithms to detect safety issues and predict drug success. This allows researchers to make more informed decisions on which drugs to continue and which to stop. AI can also be used to detect potential drug interactions and adverse reactions, saving time and money.

Insights into How AI Expedites Drug Discovery Processes

The use of AI in drug discovery and development has several benefits that expedite the process. Some of these benefits include:

1) Faster Identification of Drug Targets

AI algorithms can analyze large amounts of data from various sources, such as genetic databases and scientific literature, to identify potential drug targets. This process is much faster and more accurate than traditional methods, which involve manually searching through data.

2) More Efficient Virtual Screening

As mentioned earlier, virtual screening involves using computer algorithms to analyze large databases of chemical compounds and identify potential drug candidates. This process is much faster and more accurate than traditional methods, which involve physically testing each compound in a laboratory. This can save pharmaceutical companies time and money in the early stages of drug discovery.

3) Improved Predictions and Decision-Making

Artificial intelligence (AI) algorithms can look at data from past trials and predict how well future trials will perform. This allows drug companies to make more informed decisions on which drugs to develop and which to stop. Additionally, AI can also help identify potential safety issues and drug interactions, which can save time and money in the long run.

Examples of AI Algorithms Accelerating the Drug Development Process.

There are several examples of AI algorithms that are currently being used to accelerate drug development. Some of these include:

1) **Atomwise**

Atomwise is a company that uses AI to identify potential drug candidates. Their AI platform, AtomNet, can analyze millions of chemical compounds and identify potential drug targets in a matter of days. This is much faster and more accurate than traditional methods, which can take months or even years.

2) **Insilico Medicine**

Insilico Medicine is a company that uses AI to identify potential drug targets and develop new drugs. Their AI platform, GENTRL, can design new molecules and predict their efficacy and safety. This can save pharmaceutical companies time and money in the early stages of drug development.

3) **BenevolentAI**

BenevolentAI is a company that uses AI to analyze data from clinical trials and identify potential safety issues and drug interactions. Their AI platform, Benevolent Platform, can analyze data from various sources, such as electronic health records and scientific literature, to identify potential safety issues and drug interactions. This can help pharmaceutical companies save time and money in later phases of drug development.

Artificial intelligence (AI) is changing the way drugs are discovered and developed. With the help of AI, drug companies can find drug targets more quickly, design and create new drugs more effectively, and make better drug decisions. As AI advances, drug discovery and drug development will continue to improve, resulting in quicker and more effective cures for diseases.

Enhancing Patient Experience

In the rapidly changing world of healthcare, AI integration isn't just about diagnosis and treatment; it's about a complete transformation that puts the patient front and center. Here's a look at how AI apps are actively improving the patient experience, from AI-powered chatbots to AI-powered scheduling systems to AI-powered personalized care plans.

AI-powered Chatbots: Virtual Assistants at Your Service

Imagine a virtual assistant who answers your questions, schedules your appointments, and provides you with preliminary symptom analysis 24 hours a day, 7 days a week. That's the future of healthcare, and it's powered by AI chatbots.

These chatbots, trained on massive amounts of medical information, can answer even the most basic questions. This frees up human staff to do more complex work and reduces wait times for patients.

Chatbots can also send you personalized reminders for your medications, appointments, and follow-ups, helping you stick to your medication schedule and improve your overall health.

Scheduling Systems

The traditional phone-based appointment scheduling, often fraught with long wait times and limited options, is being replaced by intelligent AI-driven systems. By analyzing patient data and historical trends, AI-driven systems can predict appointment demand and schedule appointments in real-time. This allows for dynamic scheduling and provides patients with convenient time slots across multiple providers. Not only does this help to reduce waiting times, but it also helps to optimize resource allocation across healthcare facilities.

Personalized Care Plans

AI is revolutionizing personalized care by analyzing patient data, medical history, and genetic factors to create targeted treatment plans. This means that healthcare providers can move beyond a generic approach and provide interventions best suited for each patient. From personalized medication recommendations to preventative care, AI-driven insights can help patients take control of their healthcare journey.

Beyond the Tech: Building Trust and Empathy

While AI offers incredible potential, it is crucial to remember that technology alone cannot replace the human touch. Building trust and empathy remain cornerstones of a positive patient experience. Healthcare providers must ensure that AI tools complement, not replace, human interaction, fostering open communication and addressing patients' emotional and social needs.

Enhancing the patient experience through AI is not about replacing healthcare professionals; it's about empowering them with tools to deliver better care. By embracing AI with a human-centric approach, we can create a healthcare system that is efficient, personalized, and ultimately, more compassionate – a system where patients feel heard, understood, and empowered to participate in their well-being actively.

The future of healthcare is bright, and AI is a key driver in this transformation. As we continue to develop and integrate AI technologies, the patient experience will undoubtedly become more positive, leading to healthier individuals and a more sustainable healthcare system. Let us embrace this revolution with open arms, ensuring that AI is a powerful tool to enhance, not replace, the human connection at the heart of healthcare.

Challenges and Future Prospects

While AI holds immense promise for revolutionizing healthcare, there are hurdles to overcome:

Challenges:

- Data Privacy and Security: Protecting sensitive patient data is paramount. Robust security measures and clear regulations are needed to ensure information stays confidential.
- Algorithmic Bias: AI algorithms are only as good as the data they're trained on. Biases in training data can lead to unfair or inaccurate results. Mitigating bias requires diverse datasets and ongoing monitoring.
- Explainability and Trust: Sometimes, AI decisions can be like a black box – difficult to understand. This can make it hard for doctors and patients to trust the recommendations. More transparency in how AI reaches conclusions is crucial.
- Accessibility and Equity: Not everyone has equal access to AI-powered healthcare tools. Cost and technological limitations can create disparities. Ensuring affordability and widespread access is essential.
- Human Interaction and Empathy: AI cannot replace the human touch in healthcare. The emotional connection and empathy of a doctor are irreplaceable. AI should complement, not replace, healthcare professionals.

Future Prospects:

Despite the challenges, the future of AI in healthcare is bright:

- Personalized Medicine: AI can analyze vast amounts of patient data to create personalized treatment plans and predict individual health risks. Imagine a future where prevention is tailored to your specific needs.
- Drug Discovery and Development: AI can accelerate drug discovery by analyzing complex medical data and identifying promising drug targets. This could lead to faster development of new treatments for diseases.

- Robotic Surgery: AI-powered robots can assist surgeons with greater precision and minimal invasiveness, leading to faster recovery times for patients.
- Mental Health Support: AI chatbots and virtual therapists can offer accessible and convenient mental health support, especially in areas with limited resources.
- Continuous Learning and Improvement: AI systems can continuously learn and improve with new data. This means healthcare will constantly evolve, offering better diagnoses and treatment options over time.

The Road Ahead:

By addressing the challenges and harnessing AI's potential, we can create a future where healthcare is more personalized, efficient, and accessible for everyone. AI should be seen as a powerful tool to empower healthcare professionals and patients, ultimately leading to a healthier future for all.

Conclusion

Our exploration of AI in healthcare leaves us with remarkable insights and transformative possibilities. AI's prowess in diagnostics has ushered in an era of faster, more accurate disease detection, promising improved outcomes. The shift towards personalized medicine ensures treatments align precisely with individual needs, enhancing patient care.

Crucially, AI redefines the patient experience. From instant support through AI-driven chatbots to streamlined scheduling, patients are at the forefront of a more accessible, efficient healthcare system. However, ethical considerations, including privacy and bias, must guide our AI journey responsibly.

While challenges persist, the future holds exciting prospects. In closing, AI isn't just a technological wave—it's a transformative force shaping a healthcare future that is proactive, personalized, and compassionate. As we navigate this journey, the potential for advancements, ethical considerations, and a shared commitment to well-being opens doors to a boundless horizon of possibilities.

Chapter 8
AI and Entertainment

Grab your popcorn, people, because there's going to be a plot twist that's going to blow your mind. No, I'm not talking about a sequel or a reboot. I'm talking about an entirely new entertainment genre where robots are directors, algorithms are writers, and audiences aren't just watching it happen, they're living it. That's the rise of the AI in entertainment and it's going to be as mind-blowing as a mind-blowing plot twist by Christopher Nolan.

It's not dusty robots that dream of electric sheep. It's today's AI that's a neon-drenched showman. A digital Da Vinci creating works of art with just a few lines of words. Imagine worlds where stories change and evolve with your decisions, music moves with your mood, and art moves with your life. AI is moving us away from passive entertainment and pushing us into an interactive playground, where anything's possible.

But this isn't just about fancy tech tricks. AI is a brush dipped in human dreams, a sculptor chiseling new art forms. It's putting the power of expression in the hands of anyone with a spark of imagination and a curious mind. It's democratizing creativity, blurring the lines between artist and audience, and giving birth to unique experiences, leaving you wondering: "Did I just watch art, or did art just watch me?"

So, ditch the traditional theater seats and grab your virtual reality headset. We are on the brink of a cultural revolution that will see pixels dance, algorithms perform symphonies and the physical world merges with the digital world in ways we have never seen before.

This is not the death of art, this is the birth of art. It's a chance to step into a story, become the artist, and experience the magic of creation firsthand.

So get ready to be amazed, to be challenged, to be a part of the show. This is the age of the algorithm auteur, and the curtain's just rising. Are you ready to be the star of your AI-powered adventure?

Evolution of AI in Entertainment

Imagine a world where movie scripts are written by intelligent machines, video games respond to your mood in real-time and the next album you hear from your favorite musician is written by a computer instead of a human. This is not just a dream, this is the birth of AI in entertainment and it is happening right in front of us.

But to truly appreciate the present, we have to understand the past. The seeds of AI in entertainment were sown long ago, back in the days of clunky mainframes and pixelated Pong. Early pioneers like Joseph Weizenbaum's ELIZA, a chatbot modeled after a psychotherapist, showed us the potential for AI to tap into human emotions. Meanwhile, games like "Cybertron" (1982) experimented with AI-controlled opponents, giving players a taste of what intelligent adversaries could bring to the table.

But these advances were just the beginning. The real breakthroughs began to appear in the late 1990s and early 2000s. In 1997, Deep Blue, an artificial intelligence (AI) that plays chess, beat the world champion, Garry Kasparov. This showed that machines could outperform humans in areas that were once thought to be exclusive to our brains. In the music world, the virtual composer AIVA began creating original symphonies. This blurred the boundaries between human and machine creativity.

Then came the 2010s, the decade where AI truly hit its stride in entertainment. Natural language processing (NLP) made chatbots like Mitsuku and Cleverbot conversational masters, while advancements in computer graphics birthed hyper-realistic CGI characters indistinguishable from their flesh-and-blood counterparts. Games like "The Last of Us" showcased AI companions with near-human emotional intelligence, making gamers feel a genuine connection with their virtual teammates.

But perhaps the most significant breakthrough of all is the rise of generative AI. Tools like Google's Magenta and OpenAI's Jukebox can now compose music, write scripts, and even generate original paintings in the style of any artist. This opens up a whole new frontier for creative expression, where humans and machines collaborate to produce art that goes beyond the limitations of either alone.

The future of entertainment is brighter than a thousand suns. We're going to see more immersive, interactive experiences, more personalized content based on our personal preferences, and even new forms of art born out of human and machine collaboration. So sit back, grab a popcorn, and get ready because the show isn't over yet. The robots may be stealing the show, but they're also asking us to join in the fun. The only question is: are we ready?

AI in Music Composition and Production

Artificial Intelligence (AI) is revolutionizing the way we compose and produce music. For centuries, the human voice has been at the core of music, creating melodies and rhythms that are born from the imagination and then poured onto the instruments or even written on the staves. In recent years, however, a new actor has entered the musical world: AI. This technological genius is rapidly changing the way we create and produce music, creating exciting opportunities as well as exciting challenges.

AI as Composer: Channeling Algorithms into Art

One of the most significant ways in which AI is affecting music is through composition. AI-driven software can now analyze large collections of existing music, recognizing patterns and connections between notes, chords, and rhythms. This allows them to create new compositions, ranging from short melodies to full orchestral works. These compositions can imitate particular genres or artists and even include human-like details and emotive undertones.

Imagine that you're struggling with writer's block. You're trying to come up with a new song, but you can't seem to come up with anything new. All you can do is feed your existing work and your favorite musical influences to an AI tool. Within minutes, you'll have a kaleidoscope of new musical ideas. You can edit them, refine them, personalize them, and weave them into your creative vision. AI acts like a collaborator, the spark that ignites the human artist's flame.

However, questions arise about the nature of this collaboration. Can pure logic and calculation truly express the depth and complexity of human emotions that give music its soul? AI-generated music may be technically impressive and emotionally captivating, but some argue that it doesn't capture the raw authenticity and uniqueness that comes with the human experience.

AI as Producer: A Master of Efficiency and Innovation

Beyond composition, AI plays a crucial role in the production process. AI tools can automate the process of mixing and mastering, as well as the creation of sound design and effects. This frees up the producer's time to work on the creative aspects of the music. For example, imagine a producer is faced with a large number of audio tracks, all of which need to be handled individually. An AI assistant analyzes the audio, adjusts the levels, applies equalization, and suggests effects, making the process more efficient and ensuring a professional-sounding result.

Furthermore, AI can create new and original sound environments that would otherwise be impossible to create with conventional methods. Think of AI as a kind of virtual sonic lab where algorithms can create textures, shape waves, and create other-worldly effects that will open up sonic exploration to a whole new level.

In the middle of all this efficiency, however, there is another risk to be aware of, Over-reliance on artificial intelligence (AI) in the production process can lead to a kind of homogenization. It can also lead to a lack of individuality. Therefore, producers need to make sure that they are not using AI in such a way that they are losing out on their artistic vision as well as their sonic fingerprints.

The Human-AI Duet: A Symphony of Possibilities

The future of music in the age of AI is not about machines replacing humans, but rather about forging a powerful symphony of their combined strengths. Humans provide the spark of creativity, the emotional core, and the unique artistic vision. AI offers the tools for exploration, the tireless work ethic, and the ability to push boundaries beyond human limitations.

Imagine a world where composers collaborate with AI partners to compose melodies, producers direct AI algorithms to create custom-made soundtracks, and musicians play alongside AI-controlled virtual instruments.

A new era of creative expression is on the horizon, where technology fuels human ingenuity and unlocks new sonic realms.

However, ethical considerations need to be addressed. Questions of ownership, copyright, and the potential for AI-generated music to be exploited remain to be explored. Transparent guidelines and fair compensation models are crucial to ensure that this technological revolution benefits creators and audiences alike.

In the end, the rise of AI in music composition and production is not a threat to artistry, but rather a new frontier of creative potential. By embracing collaboration, navigating ethical challenges, and harnessing the best of both human and machine intelligence, we can create a symphony of possibilities that will resonate for generations to come.

AI in Film and Video Production

The silver screen is shimmering, and it's not just because of celluloid dreams. It's because of the magic of artificial intelligence. From creating compelling stories to creating otherworldly images, AI is shaking up every aspect of film and video creation.

It's a vision of a future where human creativity is matched only by machine creativity.

Pre-Production: Script Sculpting with AI

Imagine feeding an artificial intelligence (AI) with your wildest fantasies, your favorite movies, and a little bit of genre-shaking spice. Out of the blue, a high-quality script emerges, with plot twists as sharp as a Hitchcockian twist, and characters as nuanced as Oscar winners.

While full-blown AI-written scripts are still in the early stages of development, tools such as ScriptBook, LaMDA, and others are helping screenwriters:

- Generating story ideas and outlines: Stuck on that pesky plot hole? AI can suggest compelling narrative arcs, and character motivations, and even generate scene ideas based on your existing story threads.
- Analyzing existing scripts: AI can identify pacing issues, and inconsistencies, and even predict audience reactions, helping writers fine-tune their masterpieces before the cameras roll.
- Character development: Need a quirky sidekick or a villain dripping with malice? AI can generate detailed character profiles, complete with backstories, motivations, and even dialogue quirks.

Production

Get ready to step foot on a film set that's been infused with artificial intelligence. Drones with AI facial recognition software monitor actors' facial expressions, automatically adjusting set lights and camera angles for real-time emotional impact. In-the-moment virtual reality previsualization tools allow directors to walk through finished sets, fine-tuning scenes and visual elements before a single foundation stone is laid.

AI's effects on production include:

- Set design and virtual scouting: Forget location limitations. AI can generate photorealistic 3D environments, from alien planets to bustling cityscapes, allowing filmmakers to scout and even shoot entire scenes virtually.

- Real-time visual effects: Imagine prosthetics applied digitally, explosions rendered on the fly, or weather patterns manipulated at the touch of a button. AI-powered VFX tools are making these sci-fi dreams a reality, reducing production time and costs.
- Cinematography and shot composition: Gone are the days of endless takes. AI can analyze footage and suggest optimal camera angles, lighting setups, and even shot transitions, streamlining the filming process.

Post-Production: Editing at the Speed of Light

There's a buzz in editing suites as AI algorithms whirr through the air. Footage slides through intelligent software that automatically color-grades scenes, adds sound effects and even suggests cuts and transitions to enhance the film's emotional impact. AI is changing post-production with:

- Automated editing tasks: Repetitive edits like scene trimming, noise reduction, and color correction can be handled by AI, freeing editors to focus on the finer nuances of storytelling.
- Smart sound design: AI can analyze the emotional tone of a scene and automatically generate or recommend sound effects and music that perfectly complement the mood.
- Trailer generation: No more brainstorming for hours. AI can analyze your film and whip up a trailer that captures its essence and hooks viewers, saving valuable time and resources.

The Human-AI Duet: A Symphony of Creativity

But fear not, cinephiles, for AI, isn't here to steal the director's chair. Instead, it's a powerful tool, augmenting human creativity and allowing filmmakers to push the boundaries of storytelling like never before. Imagine:

- Personalized narratives: AI could tailor film experiences to individual viewers, dynamically adjusting the story based on their preferences and reactions.

- Interactive storytelling: Films could become living, breathing worlds where viewers can choose their paths, influencing the narrative and forging deeper connections with the characters.
- Democratizing filmmaking: AI-powered tools could make filmmaking more accessible to everyone, lowering barriers to entry and fostering a more diverse and inclusive film landscape.

The future of cinema is full of possibilities, rich in the colors of human creativity and the light of AI. It's not about robots taking over the world; it's about the symphony of human creativity, where people and machines work together to create stories that excite, captivate, and leave us in awe.

AI in Visual Arts and Design

Imagine that your paintbrush is dancing with algorithms, that robots are sculpting dreams with code, and that art galleries are filled with works of art that are born from the burning combination of human genius and machine thinking. This isn't a cyberpunk scene, it's the thrilling world of Artificial Intelligence in Visual Arts and Design.

Forget the fear of robots stealing the artist's brush. AI isn't here to replace but to reimagine. It's a powerful toolbox, a mischievous muse, and a tireless collaborator, ready to paint the canvas of visual expression in vibrant new colors.

Unleashing the Magic: AI's Artistic Arsenal

Here's a peek into the incredible tools AI brings to the party:

- AI-powered brushes: Imagine a brush that can sense your mood, mimicking the swirling frenzy of your anger or the soft caress of your joy. That's the potential of AI brushes! They learn your style, translating your feelings onto the digital canvas with every stroke.
- Algorithmic muses: If you're stuck in a rut and can't come up with new ideas, AI can be your best friend. It can help you come up with new color

palettes, create mind-blowing compositions or even create incredible creatures out of its digital dream world. No more wasting time staring at a blank sheet of paper.

- Generative engines: Feeling uninspired? Let AI be your paint mixer! It can sculpt landscapes from scratch, weave tapestries of abstract forms, or even craft eerily realistic portraits that blur the line between human and machine. Need a surreal forest? AI's got you covered.
- Style sorcerers: Want to paint like Picasso? No problem! AI can mimic any artistic style, from the swirling brushstrokes of Impressionism to the clean lines of Art Deco. It's like having a time-traveling art tutor at your fingertips.

Beyond the Canvas: AI's Design Revolution

AI isn't just for fancy art galleries; it's working its magic in the real world too:

- UI/UX Revolution: Imagine websites that adapt to your mood, interfaces that read your mind (well, not literally!), and apps that learn your preferences to create a seamless, personalized experience. AI is reshaping how we interact with the digital world, one pixel at a time.
- Fashion Forecasting: Forget crystal balls, AI is the new fashion guru! By analyzing trends, social media data, and consumer behavior, it can predict the next big thing. This helps designers stay on top of trends and avoid fashion mistakes. No more flip-flops!
- Sustainable Solutions: From upcycling waste materials to optimizing production processes, AI is helping designers create eco-conscious products with minimal environmental impact. The future of fashion is not just stylish, it's green!

Human Touch in the Age of Algorithms:

But wait, aren't robots going to dominate the art world? No, they won't. Artificial intelligence is a powerful technology, but it's just that – a technology. The real magic is the collaboration, the harmonious blend of human instinct and machine precision.

Imagine a sculptor using AI to generate 3D models of impossible shapes, then breathing life into them with their skilled hands. Or picture a graphic designer using AI to explore a million color combinations before settling on the perfect palette that evokes just the right emotion.

The future of visual art and design is an exciting partnership between man and machine. It is a world where algorithms are in love with man, pixels are in love with pixels, and the canvas extends beyond the physical to include the digital, interactive, and ever-changing landscape of our imagination.

So, the next time you see a piece of art, don't just see colors and shapes. See the potential for a new renaissance, a canvas reimagined, where the brushstrokes of AI blend seamlessly with the strokes of human genius.

Remember, AI isn't the enemy, it's the co-pilot on this wild ride of creativity. Let's buckle up and paint the world together!

AI and Virtual Reality (VR) Experiences

Imagine this: You're on the top of the world's highest peak, feeling the wind whip around you and the snow crunch beneath your virtual shoes. Or you're in the heart of Australia's Great Barrier Reef and you're surrounded by neon fish and the sun shining through the crystal clear water.

These aren't just images from a sci-fi movie; these are the mind-blowing possibilities that come to life when AI and VR collide.

Virtual Reality (VR) has already opened up the world of virtual reality to unprecedented levels of immersion. But what's behind VR's magic? What's behind the secret sauce? AI is the secret sauce. It's the little bit of magic that turns the digital world into a living, breathing world. Imagine AI as the unseen hand that manipulates the interactivity, the intelligence, within the structure of your virtual worlds.

So, how exactly does this dynamic duo work its magic? Buckle up, because we're about to dive deep into three key ways AI is revolutionizing VR experiences:

1) **Building Worlds That Dance**

Let's say you're looking for a VR experience that's more dynamic. Gone are the days of static backgrounds and robotic NPCs. Instead, AI algorithms are bringing life to VR environments by dynamically creating landscapes, weather, and even virtual character behavior.

For example, imagine exploring a jungle where AI dynamically adjusts the density of foliage based on your movements. As you explore, you'll feel a sense of discovery as you move through unseen pathways.

Or imagine climbing a mountain where AI suddenly throws in a snowstorm, forcing you to adjust your climbing strategy as you go.

This dynamic world-building forces you to constantly be on the move. Every VR experience feels fresh and exciting, like a tapestry being woven anew with each new step.

2) **Conversations that Come Alive**

Say Goodbye to Stilted, Pre-Programmed Dialogues and Hello to AI-powered Chatbots That Create Natural And Engaging Dialogues That Distinguish Between The Virtual And The Real.

Imagine walking through a medieval marketplace and bargaining with AI-driven traders whose prices and inventory change dynamically based on your past interactions and the overall rhythm of the market. Or imagine meeting a virtual friend on a lonely space journey whose personality and insights change based on your past experiences and meaningful conversations. Dynamic dialogues enhance our emotional connection with the VR world and make us feel like real participants in its narrative, not just spectators.

3) **Playgrounds Tailored Just for You**

The beauty of VR lies in its potential for complete customization. And AI is taking that to the next level by tailoring every experience to your unique preferences and skillset. Imagine training in a VR combat simulator where the AI analyzes your fighting style and adjusts the difficulty and opponent behaviors to constantly push you to your limits. Or picture learning a new language in a VR village where the AI-powered villagers speak at your pace, offer personalized feedback, and remember your previous interactions, creating a learning experience as unique as your fingerprint. This adaptive learning and individualized content ensures that every VR journey is a personal odyssey, a playground where you can explore and grow at your own pace.

Of course, this thrilling journey of AI and VR isn't without its challenges. Ethical considerations around data privacy, potential biases in AI algorithms, and the need for responsible development are critical concerns that require careful attention. We must ensure that these immersive worlds are inclusive, enriching, and free from harm.

However, despite these obstacles, the AI-driven future of VR is full of opportunities. Think of VR classrooms where students can walk with dinosaurs. Or imagine therapy sessions in VR that recreate safe environments for trauma recovery, providing unparalleled therapeutic potential. Or think of remote surgery where surgeons can save lives across continents using AI-powered VR tools.

The boundary between reality and the virtual is disappearing, and AI is painting the picture. Through ethical consciousness and sustainable development, this ground-breaking partnership has the potential to transform entertainment, education, healthcare, and even our understanding of the planet.

So put on your virtual reality headset, open your brain, and prepare to enter a world where reality is just one layer of an ever-evolving universe powered by the limitless power of AI.

The key to this technological convergence is to approach it with an open heart, a passion for discovery, and a dedication to creating a world where AI and VR create a canvas of wonder, where every pixel holds a dream waiting to come live.

AI and Personalized Content

Imagine a news app that knows what stories will grab your attention, a music streaming service that reacts to your mood, and an online shopping experience that feels like a personalized stylist's dream.

This isn't science fiction – this is the world we're entering thanks to the power of AI and its ability to personalize content.

But how does this invisible hand work? Let's peek behind the curtain and unravel the fascinating story of AI and its personalized content superpowers.

The Data Detective: Unmasking Your Preferences

It all starts with data, the lifeblood of AI. Every click, swipe, and purchase you make online leaves a digital trail. AI algorithms, like skilled detectives, sift through this vast ocean of information, piecing together your preferences and interests. They analyze your browsing history, social media activity, shopping habits, and even your location to build a detailed profile of who you are and what you like.

Think of it as a never-ending conversation you're having with the internet. AI listens carefully, noting your every whisper and translating it into a personalized content roadmap.

The Content Alchemist: Crafting Your Perfect Experience

Once your preferences are in place, AI turns into a content alchemist, using its expertise to create experiences that are specifically tailored to you. Here's how it does it:

- Newsfeed: Imagine a newsfeed devoid of irrelevant articles about celebrities you don't care about. AI analyzes your reading habits and news preferences, ensuring your feed is brimming with stories that resonate with your interests, whether it's tech trends, political commentary, or adorable animal videos.

- Music Maestro: Stop playing the same songs over and over again. AI can listen to your favorite songs, analyze your moods, and suggest new artists and genres you're going to love. It's like having your DJ who knows you better than you know yourself!
- Shopping: Say goodbye to wandering through online stores. AI analyzes your past purchases and browsing behavior, suggesting products that fit your style and needs. It's like having a virtual shopping assistant who whispers "buy this" for things you'll love and use.

The Benefits Beyond the Buzz

Personalized content isn't just about convenience and entertainment; it has real-world benefits:

- Enhanced Engagement: When content feels relevant and personal, you're more likely to engage with it, whether it's reading a news article, watching a video, or listening to a song. This translates to higher click-through rates, increased website traffic, and ultimately, happier users.
- Improved Decisions: AI can help you make informed decisions by providing personalized recommendations for products, services, or even educational resources. It's like having a trusted advisor who guides you toward choices that align with your needs and interests.
- Deeper Connections: Personalized content helps you feel more connected to brands and platforms. And when you feel like you're being heard and cared for, you're more likely to build loyalty and trust.

But wait, are there any downsides to this personalized bubble?

While AI-powered content can be incredibly useful, it's important to be aware of potential pitfalls:

- Filter Bubbles: The risk of getting trapped in an echo chamber, only seeing content that confirms your existing beliefs and biases. Remember that friend who only recommended superhero movies? You might miss out on other genres you'd enjoy.

- Privacy Concerns: Sharing data allows for personalization, but it raises concerns about how information is collected and used. Be mindful of what data you share and choose platforms with strong privacy policies.
- Ethical Dilemmas: Artificial intelligence (AI) algorithms are prone to making mistakes based on the context in which they are trained. We must make AI personalization inclusive and prevent the reinforcement of harmful stereotypes.

Looking ahead, the future of AI and personalized content is bright, with exciting possibilities:

- Immersive Experiences: Imagine personalized virtual tours of museums or customized storylines in video games, tailored to your interests and choices. It's like having a magical world adapt to your every whim.
- Health and Wellness: AI can analyze health data to offer personalized fitness plans, and dietary recommendations, and even predict potential health risks. It's like having a proactive health coach who knows your every need.
- Education Revolution: Imagine schools where AI tailors lessons to each student's learning pace and preferred style. It's like having a personal guide on your educational journey, unlocking your full potential.

AI and personalized content are not here to replace us; they're here to augment our experiences. By combining the power of AI with human creativity and ethical considerations, we can create a future where content is not just personalized, but truly enriching and meaningful. So, the next time you encounter a perfectly tailored newsfeed or a music recommendation that feels like it was made just for you, remember the AI whisperer working behind the scenes, weaving a symphony of technology and human ingenuity.

Collaborations between AI and Human Creativity

Imagine a world in which your favorite musician is no longer a one-man act, but a multi-instrumental, multi-pilot duo – themselves and their AI collaborator. Together, they compose symphonies that spin genres like pretzel seeds, weaving the symphonies of Bach and Beyoncé into a sonic symphony. This is not a far-fetched dream; this is the beginning of a new age, where human ingenuity meets the mind-boggling possibilities of AI.

Let's get away from the dystopian robots-take-over scenario. We're not talking about AI taking your artistic crown. Think of AI as an over-the-top brainstorming buddy. It's like a digital Dali, dripping ideas like paint on your canvas. It can sift through mountains of data, generate millions of variations of a melody, or even anticipate what might tug at your audience's heartstrings. Think of it as the Einsteins or Picassos of your creative life, whispering ideas in your ear and dropping artistic paint bombs on your canvas.

So, how does this creative cocktail get shaken, not stirred? Let's take a peek into different creative kitchens:

- The Pixel Palette: Imagine a painter, no longer hunched over the canvas, but instead holding a tablet in their hands like a magical brush. They sketch out a few keywords – "cyberpunk sunset, on Mars" – and the AI imagines a neon-lit cityscape, where the mountains of Mars burst into view, the sky ablaze with whirling stardust. It's not copying; it's feeding the fires of human imaginations, pushing the limits of what art can do.
- The Algorithmic Orchestra: Composers don't just sit at the piano anymore. They're jamming with AI, weaving a musical tapestry that mixes classical strings and electronic beats, just as Beethoven and Daft Punk did in the mosh pits. The AI listens to existing music, recognizes trends, and even creates new melodies, creating unexpected sonic adventures. It's a musical playground where rules are meant to be broken. Every genre is a wild card.
- The AI Quill: Writer's block is a thing of the past when you've got an AI companion by your side. They can tell you what's going on in your story, and give you character descriptions that are so real you can almost feel

their coffee breath on your skin, and even speak to you in a way that would have made Oscar Wilde blush.

They're like fast-paced beta readers on speed dial, churning out ideas as fast as they can and helping you craft a story that resonates with readers like a finely tuned bass line.

But wait, aren't robots going to take our creative jobs away? No, no, no. The robot revolution isn't here to take the place of Michelangelo and Mozart. It's here to free us from the monotonous. No more staring at an empty canvas, mesmerized by the blinking cursor. AI will take over repetitive tasks, endless brainstorming, and the heavy lifting of research so that humans can focus on the heart of their work. It'll be like having an unstoppable assistant, always on hand to bring coffee, inspiration, and perhaps even a new perspective.

Of course, this brave new world comes with its challenges. We need to ensure that AI doesn't homogenize creativity, but instead, amplifies diverse voices and perspectives. We need to address questions of ownership and authorship in a world where humans and machines co-create. But with careful navigation, these challenges can be overcome.

There's no denying the potential of this collaboration. It's not just about fancy gadgets; it's about rewriting the rules of what's possible. Exploring new creative possibilities, going beyond the canvas and score sheet, and working hand in hand with our silicon friends. A future where art isn't just about people, it's a symphony of humanity and machines, a symphony of imagination that leaves us breathless.

So, the next time you see a robot with a paintbrush or an AI humming a tune, don't be afraid. Instead, embrace collaboration, unleash creativity, and prepare for a new era where humans and AI work together to paint the future, one brilliant stroke at a time.

And that's just the tip of the iceberg. Let's drink to the future where creativity is limitless and the only limitation is our imaginations and, God only knows, the brains of our AI friends.

Societal Impact and Ethical Considerations

Artificial intelligence (AI) is rapidly transforming the entertainment industry, bringing both exciting possibilities and ethical concerns. Let's delve into how AI is impacting society and the questions we need to ask.

On the Positive Side...

- Enhanced Experiences: AI personalizes entertainment. Imagine recommendation systems suggesting movies you'll love or music that fits your mood. AI can also power immersive experiences in virtual reality (VR) and augmented reality (AR), making us feel like we're part of the action.
- Creative Spark: AI can be a creative collaborator. Scriptwriting tools can help generate ideas, while AI-powered music composers can create unique soundtracks. This can accelerate the creative process and even inspire new artistic directions.
- Accessibility Boost: AI can make entertainment more accessible. Imagine voice-controlled interfaces for those with physical limitations or AI-generated subtitles for a wider audience.

But There's a Flip Side...

- Job Displacement: AI automation might replace some jobs in entertainment, like special effects artists or background performers. We need to ensure a smooth transition and equip people with skills for the evolving industry.
- The Bias Problem: AI systems trained on biased data can perpetuate stereotypes on race, gender, or other factors. This can limit representation and create unfair portrayals in entertainment.
- Deepfake Dilemma: AI can create realistic-looking fake videos (deepfakes) that could be used to spread misinformation or damage reputations. We need safeguards to ensure authenticity and prevent misuse.

Ethical Considerations for the Future

- Transparency: Being clear about how AI is used in entertainment builds trust. Audiences should know if they're interacting with an AI or a human actor.
- Data Responsibility: Data used to train AI systems needs to be diverse and unbiased. This ensures fair representation and reduces the risk of discriminatory portrayals.
- Human Control: AI should be a tool, not a replacement for human creativity. The entertainment industry thrives on human imagination and storytelling, and AI should complement, not replace these aspects.

By addressing these societal impacts and ethical considerations, we can ensure AI enhances entertainment for everyone, fostering creativity, inclusivity, and responsible innovation.

Future Trends and Speculations

AI's hold on the entertainment industry is only getting stronger. Buckle up as we explore some mind-bending trends and speculations about what the future might hold:

The Rise of the AI Co-Stars and Storytellers

- Interactive Characters: Imagine AI-powered characters in games or movies that respond to your choices, creating a truly personalized narrative experience.
- AI Directors and Writers? AI could analyze vast amounts of data to craft stories tailored to specific audiences, or even co-write scripts with human screenwriters, bringing fresh perspectives and unexpected twists.

Hyper-Personalization: Entertainment Just for You

- Mood-Adaptive Stories: AI could curate shows or movies that dynamically adjust to your mood. Feeling down? An AI might recommend a light comedy. Feeling pumped? Get ready for an action flick with a perfectly tailored soundtrack generated by AI.

- The Learning Experience: AI could track your viewing habits and preferences, not just recommending content, but also creating personalized learning experiences. Imagine educational games or documentaries that adapt to your pace and interests.

Breaking Down Barriers: A More Inclusive Future

- AI-Powered Language Translation: AI could translate movies and shows in real-time, removing language barriers and making entertainment truly global.
- Accessibility Revolution: AI could create audio descriptions, subtitles, and sign language interpretation for all forms of entertainment, ensuring everyone has an equal opportunity to enjoy it.

The Blur Between Reality and Entertainment

- Hyper-Realistic VR Experiences: Imagine AI-powered VR experiences that feel indistinguishable from reality. Step into a historical event or explore a fantastical world, all thanks to AI's ability to create ever-more immersive simulations.
- The Rise of AI-Generated Influencers: We might see AI-powered virtual celebrities with massive followings. But how will we know if we're interacting with a real person or a sophisticated AI creation?

Remember, these are just speculations. AI development is rapid, and the future is unwritten. However, by considering these possibilities, we can ensure AI in entertainment enhances creativity, fosters empathy, and pushes the boundaries of what's possible.

Conclusion

AI is revolutionizing entertainment, offering a treasure trove of possibilities – from personalized experiences to groundbreaking storytelling. However, ethical considerations regarding bias, job displacement, and responsible use of technology require careful attention. By embracing AI's potential while addressing its challenges, we can shape a future where entertainment is not only captivating but also inclusive, innovative, and beneficial for society as a whole. This exciting journey with AI in entertainment has just begun, and the possibilities are truly limitless.

Chapter 9
AI and Environment

Imagine a world where robots roam forests, not to chop down trees, but to identify poachers. Imagine smart grids predicting energy demands, seamlessly switching between solar and wind power. Imagine farms maximizing yields while minimizing water usage, guided by the invisible hand of AI. This isn't science fiction; it's the reality unfolding as Artificial Intelligence (AI) embraces its role as a champion for the environment.

But before we delve into its heroic acts, let's dispel the myth of AI as a magical green genie. AI isn't an instant solution, but rather a powerful tool waiting to be wielded. Just like a hammer in the wrong hands can damage, AI, without careful consideration, can exacerbate environmental issues. So, what makes AI unique in this fight for our planet?

Think Big, Act Small: AI's Superpowers for a Sustainable Future

Imagine analyzing mountains of data – climate patterns, soil quality, animal migration – in seconds. With its superhuman analytical abilities, AI can:

- Predict and prepare: AI models can forecast weather patterns, anticipate droughts, and even predict wildfires, allowing communities to proactively prepare and minimize damage.
- Optimize resources: From smart grids that manage energy requirements to farms that use AI-driven sensors for focused irrigation, AI optimizes

resource efficiency and reduces waste and pollution.

- Monitor and protect: AI-powered drones scan vast landscapes for illegal logging or poaching, while intelligent cameras track endangered species, providing valuable data for conservation efforts.
- Boost efficiency: Whether it's designing sustainable buildings or optimizing transportation systems, AI algorithms can recommend solutions that reduce our environmental impact.

This is just a taste of what AI can do. But the key is to harness it in the right way. We must tackle ethical issues, make sure everyone has access to these tools, and focus on green solutions, not just big business.

Why AI Matters: A Necessity, Not a Luxury

Climate change, biodiversity loss, and resource depletion – these challenges require innovative solutions, and AI offers a unique edge. Here's why:

- The scale of the problem demands it: Traditional methods are often too slow and resource-intensive to tackle complex environmental issues. AI's ability to analyze massive datasets and suggest data-driven solutions can accelerate progress.
- Precision is key: AI can personalize solutions to specific contexts, whether optimizing fertilizer use for each field or tailoring conservation strategies to unique ecosystems.
- Speed is of the essence: With environmental threats escalating, we need solutions that can adapt and evolve quickly. AI's capacity for continuous learning allows it to keep pace with changing needs.

In this battle for our planet, we need to act together. By using AI correctly, we can build a future where AI and nature co-exist, creating a sustainable future for future generations. So, what are you waiting for? Let's make AI the champion of the environment!

AI in Climate Monitoring

Imagine Earth, our vibrant blue marble, constantly whispering secrets about its health. But these whispers come in the form of massive datasets – satellite images, sensor readings, weather patterns – too complex for humans to decipher alone. Enter the mighty AI, the superhero of climate monitoring, ready to translate these whispers into actionable insights.

Satellite Data Analysis: Seeing the Bigger Picture

Think of satellites as millions of tiny eyes watching over our planet. They capture incredible amounts of data, but analyzing it all? That's where AI steps in. Imagine a super-powered brain sifting through mountains of images, identifying patterns invisible to the human eye. AI can:

- Track temperature changes: Like a heat map for the Earth, AI can identify areas warming faster than others, helping us understand climate trends and predict future impacts.
- Monitor sea level rise: By analyzing satellite images of coastlines, AI can measure sea level changes with incredible accuracy, helping coastal communities prepare for rising waters.
- Spot forest fires: AI can scan vast areas for signs of smoke and flames, alerting firefighters much faster than traditional methods, saving lives and precious ecosystems.

Predictive Modeling: Weather Woes, Be Gone!

Remember that movie where a butterfly's wing flap in one place causes a hurricane in another? Well, weather is complex, but AI is learning to predict it better than ever. By analyzing historical data, weather patterns, and even social media trends, AI can:

- Forecast extreme weather events: From floods to droughts, AI can predict these events with more accuracy and lead time, allowing communities to prepare and minimize damage.

- Identify climate change "hotspots": AI can also identify the areas that are most at risk of extreme weather events, allowing governments to better allocate resources and create tailored adaptation plans.
- Optimize renewable energy production: By predicting wind and solar patterns, AI can help maximize energy output from renewable sources, making them more reliable and efficient.

Monitoring Deforestation: Saving Our Green Lungs

Forests are vital for our planet, but deforestation is a major threat. AI is becoming a powerful tool to:

- Detecting illegal logging: By analyzing satellite images and identifying unusual patterns, AI can help authorities catch illegal loggers before they cause significant damage.
- Monitor forest health: AI can track changes in vegetation cover, identifying areas affected by disease, pests, or droughts, allowing for early intervention and conservation efforts.
- Support sustainable forestry: By analyzing data on forest growth and carbon sequestration, AI can help develop sustainable forestry practices that balance economic needs with environmental protection.

But AI isn't magic. It needs our help!

While AI is a powerful tool, it's not a silver bullet. Here's what we need to do:

- Invest in research and development: We need to continue improving AI algorithms and training them on even larger datasets to increase their accuracy and effectiveness.
- Address ethical concerns: We need to ensure AI is used responsibly and transparently, considering potential biases and ensuring it benefits everyone, not just certain groups.
- Collaboration is key: Scientists, policymakers, and AI experts need to

work together to develop and implement AI solutions that are effective, sustainable, and equitable.

The solution to climate change is a shared responsibility, and AI is becoming an invaluable asset. By using its power in the right way, we can better understand our planet, anticipate and reduce risks, and create a more resilient world for everyone. So, let's work together with AI, not only to monitor climate change but to make a difference!

Sustainable Agriculture

Imagine fields that whisper their needs, crops that call for help when sick, and robots that work tirelessly alongside farmers, not replacing them, but amplifying their skills. This isn't a sci-fi fantasy, but a glimpse into the exciting world of sustainable agriculture powered by artificial intelligence (AI). So, grab your virtual pitchfork and join us on a journey where technology meets tradition, creating a greener, more productive future for our food!

Precision Farming: Every Drop Counts

Traditionally, farming has been a bit like throwing seeds and hoping for the best. But what if we could treat each plant like an individual, giving it exactly what it needs, no more, no less? Enter precision farming – AI's secret weapon for resource optimization. Here's how it works:

- Soil sensors whisper secrets: Imagine tiny spies buried in the soil, constantly sending data about moisture, nutrients, and even pest presence. AI analyzes this data, creating detailed maps that help farmers apply fertilizer and water only where needed, saving resources and money.
- Drones become digital farmers: Picture these buzzing robots not just capturing cool aerial shots, but actually surveying fields, identifying stressed plants, and even spraying targeted doses of pesticides, minimizing waste and environmental impact.

- Robots lend a helping hand: Forget Rosie the maid, think of Rosie the robot farmer! These tireless machines can weed, plant, and harvest with incredible accuracy, freeing up farmers for more strategic tasks and reducing manual labor fatigue.

Crop Disease Detection: Saving Our Food Heroes

Just like us, plants get sick too. But unlike us, they can't call the doctor (yet!). This is where AI becomes a champion crop defender:

- Early detection is key: AI-powered apps analyze images captured by smartphones or drones, identifying diseases at their earliest stages before they spread and devastate yields. This allows farmers to take swift action, minimizing losses and ensuring healthy harvests.
- Predictive power prevents outbreaks: By analyzing historical data and weather patterns, AI can predict disease outbreaks before they happen. Farmers can then take preventive measures, like using resistant crop varieties or applying targeted fungicides, protecting their crops and ensuring food security.
- Precision treatment, less waste: Instead of spraying entire fields with chemicals, AI can pinpoint infected plants and recommend targeted treatment, minimizing pesticide use and protecting beneficial insects. This protects both the environment and human health.

But it's not all sunshine and robots...

While AI in sustainable agriculture holds immense promise, there are challenges:

- Cost and accessibility: Not all farmers have access to expensive technology or the training to use it effectively. We need solutions that are affordable and user-friendly for all.
- Data privacy and security: Farmers' data is valuable, and its security is paramount. Robust data protection measures are crucial to building trust

and encouraging adoption.

- Ethical considerations: As AI takes on more roles in agriculture, it's essential to ensure it benefits everyone, not just large corporations. We need ethical frameworks to guide development and ensure equitable access to technology.

The Future is Green(er) with AI

Despite the challenges, AI's potential to transform agriculture sustainably is undeniable. By working together, scientists, farmers, policymakers, and tech companies can create a future where AI empowers farmers to grow more food with fewer resources, protects our environment, and ensures food security for everyone. So, let's embrace the future of smart farming, not with fear, but with the hope that together, we can cultivate a more sustainable and bountiful world for generations to come.

Conservation and Wildlife Protection

Imagine a future where cameras keep a close eye on endangered species, AI tricks poachers into thinking twice before they attack, and algorithms lead the way to save disappearing habitats. It's not a dream, it's the thrilling future of wildlife conservation and AI-powered conservation. Join us on an adventure into the wild, where technology is a lifesaver for our planet's most endangered creatures.

Eyes in the Sky: AI-powered Cameras for Endangered Species

Imagine a hidden camera in the jungle, not just capturing blurry footage, but recognizing a specific jaguar by its unique spots. This is the magic of AI-powered cameras, revolutionizing how we monitor endangered species:

- Seeing through the chaos: Traditional cameras capture everything, making it difficult to identify specific animals. AI analyzes footage, recognizing individual animals based on their unique features, like a tiger's stripes or a panda's markings. This allows researchers to track populations, study behavior, and identify threats more effectively.

- 24/7 watch: Unlike human observers, AI cameras never sleep. They can monitor vast areas continuously, capturing vital data on animal movements, breeding patterns, and even interactions with their environment. This data helps researchers understand species' needs and develop targeted conservation strategies.
- Citizen science for all: AI-powered camera systems can be deployed at lower costs than traditional methods, making them accessible to citizen scientists and local communities. This empowers people to contribute to conservation efforts, fostering a sense of ownership and responsibility.

Poachers Beware: Predictive Analytics for Prevention

Poaching is a major threat to wildlife, but AI is becoming a formidable opponent:

- Predicting poaching hotspots: By analyzing historical data on poaching incidents, weather patterns, and animal movements, AI can identify areas at high risk for poaching activity. This allows rangers to focus their patrols on these hotspots, making them more efficient and effective in deterring poachers.
- Real-time alerts and tracking: AI-powered systems can analyze camera footage in real time, identifying suspicious activity and alerting rangers immediately. This allows for swift intervention, preventing poachers from harming animals and escaping with illegal wildlife products.

Habitat Heroes: AI-Driven Insights for Preservation

Protecting animal homes is crucial for their survival, and AI is offering a helping hand:

- Mapping essential habitats: AI can analyze satellite imagery and environmental data to identify areas critical for specific species. This helps conservationists prioritize land acquisition and restoration efforts, ensuring animals have the resources they need to thrive.
- Predicting habitat changes: Climate change and human activities are constantly altering landscapes. AI can predict how these changes will impact animal habitats, allowing conservationists to develop proactive strategies to mitigate negative effects and protect crucial areas.
- Optimizing resource management: AI can analyze data on land use, animal populations, and resource availability to help develop sustainable management plans for protected areas. This ensures resources are used efficiently, benefiting both wildlife and local communities.

A Future Filled with Hope

The future for conservation and wildlife conservation with AI is clear. By using technology in the right way, we can build a world where wildlife is thriving, habitats are safeguarded and future generations will inherit a planet full of life.

So, let's use AI as a force for good, not just for monitoring and conservation, but for inspiring and empowering us to be true stewards of the world's wildlife.

Don't forget that the future of the planet's most valuable creatures is in our hands. AI can shine a light on a brighter, greener tomorrow.

Pollution Monitoring and Control

Pollution is everywhere. We breathe it, we drink it, we walk on it. It's everywhere. But there's a new hero on the planet, and it's called AI.
By harnessing the power of AI, we're not just monitoring pollution. We're creating smarter solutions to control pollution and protect the planet.

So, what are you waiting for? Join us on a journey where technology is the ultimate pollution killer!

Air-mazing Sensors Network: Keeping an Eye on the Breath We Breathe

Imagine tiny sentinels scattered across cities, constantly monitoring the air we breathe. These are sensor networks, and AI is their brain:

- Real-time air quality reports: Gone are the days of waiting for monthly air quality reports. Sensor networks provide real-time data on pollutants like ozone, particulate matter, and nitrogen oxides. AI analyzes this data, providing instant updates on air quality and pinpointing areas needing immediate attention.
- Identifying pollution sources: From traffic jams to industrial chimneys, AI can use sensor data to identify the major sources of air pollution. This empowers authorities to target specific polluters and enforce regulations more effectively.
- Predicting smog alerts: Just like predicting the weather, AI can analyze trends and historical data to predict smog events before they happen. This allows authorities to issue early warnings and implement temporary measures to protect public health.

Turning Water Woes into Water Wins: AI for Cleaner H2O

Our rivers and oceans deserve better than being dumping grounds. Here's how AI is cleaning up its act:

- Smart water quality monitoring: From sensors deployed in rivers to satellites scanning vast oceans, AI analyzes data on parameters like dissolved oxygen, bacteria levels, and chemical pollutants. This helps identify and tackle contamination early on, preventing major environmental damage.
- Optimizing wastewater treatment: Traditional wastewater treatment plants are energy-intensive. AI can analyze data on water flow, pollutant levels, and energy consumption to optimize treatment processes, making them more efficient and sustainable.

Waste Not, Want Not: AI's Magical Waste Transformation

Waste isn't waste; it's just misplaced resources! AI is showing us how to turn trash into treasure:

- Smart waste sorting: Robots equipped with AI and computer vision can sort waste with incredible accuracy, separating recyclables from organic waste and hazardous materials. This improves recycling rates and diverts tons of waste from landfills.
- Predicting waste generation: By analyzing data on consumption patterns and demographics, AI can predict how much waste different communities will generate. This helps authorities plan better waste management infrastructure and optimize collection routes.
- Transforming waste into energy: AI can analyze the composition of waste and suggest the most efficient ways to convert it into valuable biofuels or energy. This reduces reliance on fossil fuels and creates a circular economy where waste becomes a resource.

The Fight Continues: Challenges and Opportunities

While AI offers immense potential, challenges remain:

- Data privacy and security: Sensitive data collected by sensors and networks needs robust protection. Building trust and transparency is crucial for widespread adoption.
- Infrastructure and accessibility: Deploying AI in remote areas requires reliable internet access and data storage infrastructure. Bridging the digital divide is essential for equitable access to solutions.
- Sustainable development: We must ensure AI solutions benefit everyone, not just corporations. Ethical considerations and inclusive development are paramount.

From Patrol to Guardianship: Building a Brighter Future

Despite the challenges, there is a bright future for pollution monitoring and control using AI. By collaborating with scientists, policymakers, and tech companies, we can create and deploy AI solutions that are efficient, sustainable, and fair. Let's move beyond simply patrolling for pollution and become true guardians of our planet, using AI to build a cleaner, healthier world for generations to come. Remember, the fight against pollution is a collective effort, and AI can be our powerful ally in this epic battle. So let's work together, innovate, and create a new era where sustainability is the new normal!

Renewable Energy Optimization

Imagine a world in which the sun's rays, the wind's breath, and the ocean's tides work together to power our homes, industries, and transportation. It's not just a fantasy, it's the future. Renewable energy is the promise of the future, and its secret weapon is artificial intelligence (AI). Get ready to dive into the exciting world of how AI optimizes renewable energy, rendering it cleaner, more cost-effective, and more dependable than ever before.

The Challenge of Renewables

Renewable energy sources like solar, wind, and geothermal are abundant and eco-friendly, but they have a catch: they're intermittent. The sun doesn't always shine, the wind doesn't always blow, and the earth's heat isn't always readily accessible. This inconsistency makes it difficult to integrate them seamlessly into the traditional power grid, which relies on predictable and constant sources like coal or natural gas.

Enter the AI Hero: Predicting, Optimizing, and Automating

This is where AI swoops in like a superhero, wielding its superpowers of data analysis, machine learning, and automation. Here's how AI is changing the game:

- Predicting the Unpredictable: AI algorithms can analyze vast amounts of weather data, historical generation patterns, and even satellite imagery to predict with incredible accuracy when the sun will shine, the wind will pick up, or the tides will surge. This allows energy providers to optimize their systems and prepare for fluctuations in power generation.
- Optimizing Every Watt: AI can analyze real-time data from individual wind turbines, solar panels, or geothermal plants to identify inefficiencies and suggest adjustments. This could involve tilting solar panels towards the sun for maximum absorption, adjusting turbine blades for optimal wind capture, or fine-tuning geothermal plant operations.
- Automating the Grid: AI can automate tasks like switching between different renewable sources, storing excess energy in batteries, and even trading energy on the grid based on real-time demand and price fluctuations. This makes the grid more responsive and flexible, ensuring a smooth and stable flow of clean energy.

Beyond Efficiency: The Ripple Effect of AI-powered Renewables

The benefits of AI-optimized renewables extend far beyond just generating clean electricity. Here are some exciting possibilities:

- Smarter Cities: AI can help cities manage their energy consumption by predicting demand and optimizing distribution networks, leading to reduced energy waste and lower costs.
- Empowered Communities: Imagine individuals with rooftop solar panels selling their excess energy back to the grid, creating a decentralized and democratic energy system. AI can facilitate this by managing microtransactions and ensuring fair pricing.
- Boosting Sustainability: By making renewables more efficient and cost-effective, AI can accelerate the transition away from fossil fuels, leading to cleaner air, reduced greenhouse gas emissions, and a healthier planet.

Remember, this is just the beginning of the story. As AI technology continues to evolve, its impact on renewable energy will only become more profound and transformative.

Challenges and Ethical Considerations

Imagine a world where AI drones scour forests for poachers and monitor endangered species, or robots sort recyclables to maximize resource recovery. There's no denying that AI has the potential to transform the way we protect the planet, but like any powerful technology, it also comes with challenges and ethical questions.

In this section, we will dive deep into this exciting yet complex world, looking at both the huge potential and the challenges AI poses to the environment.

Unintended Consequences

Imagine an artificial intelligence (AI) system that analyzes data to determine the best way to irrigate crops. After analyzing the data, the system automatically adjusts the water flow to maximize the crop's yield. Sounds like a win-win for agriculture, right? But what if that AI system accidentally drains groundwater reserves, resulting in a water shortage in the future? These are just a few of the consequences that can occur when complex AI systems interact with the delicate balance of the environment.

Another concern is the potential for overfitting, where an AI trained on specific data struggles to adapt to real-world variations. Imagine a system trained to detect deforestation from satellite images. It might excel at identifying clear-cut areas but miss subtle changes, like selective logging or canopy thinning. Such blind spots could lead to underestimating environmental threats.

Ethical quandaries: Where AI and morality collide

In addition to the technical challenges, artificial intelligence in the environment raises many ethical questions. One of the biggest concerns is that AI algorithms may be trained on data sets that unknowingly reflect social biases. For example, imagine a system designed to detect polluters. If the system is trained on data that has a history of bias against a particular industry or community, it could unfairly penalize them, further exacerbating existing inequalities.

Another ethical issue is one of transparency and clarity. AI systems often operate as "black boxes," with decisions made in mysterious ways that make it hard to hold them to account for potential damage or make sure they're in line with our ethical values.

For example, imagine an AI system that makes decisions about how to allocate resources: how can you trust it to prioritize environmental sustainability or social justice if the reasoning behind its decisions is unclear?

Navigating the Tightrope: Solutions and Safeguards

Despite these challenges, the potential benefits of AI in the environment are too significant to ignore. So, how do we move forward responsibly? Here are some key steps:

- Data Diversity and Quality: Ensure training data is diverse and representative, mitigating bias and ensuring the AI system can handle real-world complexities.
- Transparency and Explainability: Develop AI models that are more transparent and explainable, allowing humans to understand and audit their decisions.
- Human Oversight and Accountability: Maintain human oversight and accountability throughout the AI development and deployment process.
- Ethical Guidelines and Frameworks: Establish clear ethical guidelines and frameworks for AI development and use in environmental applications.
- Public Engagement and Dialogue: Foster open dialogue and public engagement to ensure AI aligns with societal values and environmental goals.

The road to a green future is bumpy. But by recognizing the challenges and having an honest conversation about ethics, we can use AI to build a greener, fairer future for everyone. Keep in mind that AI is a powerful tool, and like all powerful tools, its influence depends on the people who use it. Let's use AI wisely and make the green dream a reality, not an oxymoron.

So, let's take this journey together. Let's face the challenges head-on with a shared focus on environmental good and ethical good.

Conclusion

The relationship between AI and the environment is a complex dance of potential and peril. AI offers a powerful toolkit for understanding, monitoring, and optimizing our environment. From precision agriculture to climate change prediction, AI can revolutionize how we interact with the Earth. However, the environmental impact of AI itself, its potential for misuse, and the ethical considerations of large-scale data collection must be addressed. By fostering responsible development and prioritizing sustainability, we can ensure that AI becomes a force for positive environmental change

Chapter 10

AI and You: How to Adapt and Thrive in the AI Era

AI: The New Landscape

Imagine a world in which your morning commute is controlled by a driverless car, your doctor uses Artificial Intelligence (AI) for faster and more accurate diagnoses, and your favorite streaming service automatically curates your favorite shows based on your mood.

It's not just a dream. AI is changing the way we live, work, and communicate. It's changing the way we consume information and entertain ourselves. And it's changing us fast.

Looking ahead, the potential for AI's impact is even more astounding. Imagine cities with intelligent traffic management systems that eliminate congestion, or educational platforms that personalize learning for each student. While anxieties about job displacement and responsible AI development are valid, the future holds exciting possibilities for human-machine collaboration that can propel us toward a brighter future.

But let's not get lost in futuristic visions just yet. AI's presence is already deeply felt. Think about the virtual assistants like Siri or Alexa seamlessly integrated into your smart home, or the recommendation algorithms that shape your online shopping experience. Social media platforms leverage AI to personalize feeds and target advertising while ride-sharing apps utilize

AI algorithms to optimize routes and pricing. These are just a few examples of how AI is subtly, yet profoundly, influencing our present.

The Rise of the Human-Machine Partnership

Forget the dystopian visions of robots taking over the world. The future of AI is not about machines replacing humans, but rather humans and machines working together as a powerful team. This collaboration, known as the human-machine partnership, is already yielding incredible results and holds immense potential for the future.

Think of a surgeon performing a delicate operation, their skill augmented by an AI that analyzes real-time data and provides critical insights. Or a scientist conducting groundbreaking research, with AI sifting through mountains of data to identify patterns and accelerate discoveries. These are just a few examples of how AI is already amplifying human capabilities.

The key to this successful partnership lies in understanding the unique strengths of both humans and machines. AI excels at processing vast amounts of data and identifying patterns, but it lacks the creativity, emotional intelligence, and complex problem-solving skills that humans possess. By combining these strengths, we can achieve far more than we could alone.

So, how can you equip yourself to thrive in this era of human-machine collaboration? The answer lies in honing your uniquely human skills. Sharpen your critical thinking, communication, and social intelligence. These are the skills that AI simply can't replicate and will be highly sought after in the future workforce.

But collaboration also requires an understanding of your AI partner. By learning about AI's limitations and how to communicate effectively with it, you can become an "AI whisperer," ensuring a smooth and productive partnership.

Equipping Yourself for the AI Age

The work landscape is constantly evolving, and the rise of AI is accelerating this change. While anxieties about job displacement are natural, the truth is that the AI age isn't about humans being replaced by machines. Instead, it's about embracing AI as a powerful tool and developing the skills to thrive alongside it.

The key is to sharpen your human edge. AI excels at crunching data and identifying patterns, but it doesn't have the creativity, emotional intelligence, or nuanced problem-solving skills that make us who we are. Strengthen your critical thinking skills:

Analyze information, recognize what's wrong, and make informed decisions. Improve communication skills: Express ideas clearly, work well together and build meaningful connections. Emotional intelligence: Understand and manage your emotions. Recognize and respond to others' emotions.

Furthermore, building a complementary skillset alongside your human strengths is crucial. Data analysis, the ability to interpret and draw insights from data, is a valuable skill in the AI age. Clear and concise communication remains essential for collaborating with AI and humans alike.

Lifelong learning is no longer a luxury, but a necessity. Embrace online courses, boot camps, and certifications to stay relevant in the evolving job market. Develop a personalized learning plan that focuses on the skills most in demand for your field. Remember, the ability to learn and adapt will be key to navigating the ever-changing landscape powered by AI.

Thriving in the AI Era

The rise of AI presents not just challenges, but incredible opportunities. By embracing a proactive approach and developing the right skill set, you can not only survive but thrive in this exciting new era.

1) Becoming an AI Whisperer

The future of work demands an understanding of your AI partner. Learn about AI's limitations – it can't replace human creativity or handle complex ethical dilemmas. Develop clear communication skills to effectively convey your goals and expectations to AI. By becoming an "AI whisperer," you'll be well-positioned to collaborate productively with this powerful tool.

2) Charting Your AI-Powered Career Path

The AI era isn't about the end of jobs, but rather a transformation. New job opportunities are emerging in fields like AI development, data science, and cybersecurity. Existing careers will adapt, requiring new skill sets to work alongside AI. For example, a marketing professional might learn to leverage AI for targeted advertising campaigns.

Explore the possibilities – research emerging AI-driven professions that align with your interests and skills. Consider taking online courses or certifications to bridge any skill gaps. Remember, lifelong learning is key to staying relevant in the AI-powered workforce.

3) Humanity & AI: A Force for Good

Imagine a world where AI tackles global challenges alongside us. AI can analyze vast datasets to predict and address climate change or assist in developing personalized medicine to eradicate diseases. The potential for positive change through human-AI collaboration is limitless.

4) Embrace the Future

The key to thriving in the AI era lies in a positive and proactive approach. Don't shy away from AI – embrace it as a powerful tool for progress. By equipping yourself with the right skills and fostering a collaborative mindset, you can shape the future of AI and ensure it serves humanity's best interests.

Chapter 11
How to Embrace AI for Everyone

AI has gone from being a far-fetched concept to being an integral part of our day-to-day lives. We rely on AI to make sense of the world around us, from the weather forecast on our AI-enabled smartphones to the customized music playlists that keep us going during our long commutes.

As AI becomes more pervasive, it can also become a source of unease and fear. Fear of job loss, fear of privacy invasion, fear of losing our jobs, fear of being taken advantage of, fear of being left behind, fear of not being able to do our best to make the most of the incredible opportunities that AI has to bring to our lives and society.

This chapter aims to be your guide on this journey of embracing AI. Here, we'll debunk some myths, showcase how AI can be a powerful tool, and offer practical steps to incorporate it into your daily routine. We'll also explore ways to build a basic understanding of AI and participate in shaping its responsible development. By the end, you'll be equipped to navigate the exciting world of AI with confidence and optimism.

Overcoming the Fear Factor

Fear often arises from the unknown. When it comes to AI, some worry about robots taking over our jobs or superintelligent machines surpassing human control. These anxieties, while understandable, paint an inaccurate picture. Let's dispel the myth of AI as a replacement for humans and instead see it as a powerful collaborator.

The truth is, AI excels at handling vast amounts of data and repetitive tasks, freeing us to focus on our uniquely human strengths: creativity, critical thinking, and social intelligence. Imagine a world where AI tackles the monotonous paperwork, allowing doctors to spend more time with patients. Or envision AI personalizing education, tailoring lessons to each student's learning style. AI becomes a tool that empowers us to achieve more, not a competitor vying for our jobs.

The benefits of AI are already evident in many aspects of our lives. Personalized medicine uses AI to analyze patient data and predict potential health issues. Educational tools powered by AI can adapt to individual learning needs, creating a more engaging and effective learning experience. Accessibility tools like voice recognition software and virtual assistants are breaking down barriers for people with disabilities, fostering a more inclusive world.

The key takeaway? Don't fear AI. Embrace it as a partner with the potential to make our lives easier, healthier, and more fulfilling. In the next section, we'll explore how you can start leveraging AI in your daily routine.

Embracing AI in Your Daily Life

AI is already embedded in many aspects of our lives, and sometimes we don't even realize it. Take a look at when you last used your phone. There's a good chance that AI was working in the background, powering functions like:

- Voice assistants: Siri, Alexa, and Google Assistant use AI to understand your voice commands and complete tasks, from setting alarms to playing music.
- Smart recommendations: Streaming services and online retailers use AI to suggest content and products tailored to your preferences.
- Personalized news feeds: Social media platforms leverage AI to curate news stories relevant to your interests, keeping you informed and engaged.

But AI's potential extends far beyond entertainment. Here are some ways you can actively leverage AI to boost your productivity and enrich your daily routine:

- Productivity powerhouses: Utilize AI-powered task management apps that prioritize your to-do list and automate repetitive tasks.
- Language learning made easy: Explore interactive apps powered by AI that personalize language learning journeys and make the process more engaging and effective.
- Tailored news consumption: Stay informed with AI-driven news aggregators that filter information overload and deliver stories relevant to your professional and personal interests.
- Smart home, happy home: Explore smart home devices controlled by AI that adjust thermostats, manage lighting, and even optimize your home security system.

The key to embracing AI lies not just in using these tools but in understanding how they work. This basic knowledge empowers you to make informed choices about the information you share and the algorithms that influence your decisions.

In the next section, we'll delve into building a foundational understanding of AI to empower you to become a more informed and engaged participant in the AI revolution.

Building Your AI Knowledge Base

AI can feel like a complex and jargon-filled field. But fear not! Building a basic understanding of AI doesn't require a PhD in computer science. Here's how to equip yourself with the knowledge to navigate the world of AI with confidence:

- Understanding the Types of AI: There are different flavors of AI, each with its strengths. Machine learning, for example, allows AI to learn from data without explicit programming. Natural language processing enables AI to understand and generate human language, powering features like chatbots and virtual assistants. Familiarize yourself with these core concepts to gain a deeper appreciation of AI's capabilities.

- Learning Resources at Your Fingertips: The internet is brimming with resources to jumpstart your AI education. Online courses, informative articles, and engaging TED Talks can break down complex concepts into digestible chunks. Explore platforms like Coursera, EdX, or Khan Academy for introductory courses on AI and machine learning.
- Focus on Building a Foundation, Not Becoming an Expert: Don't feel pressured to become an AI guru. The goal is to develop a basic understanding that empowers you to make informed choices about the AI-powered tools you use. By understanding the core concepts, you can ask intelligent questions and participate in discussions about the impact of AI on society.

Remember, the journey of learning is an ongoing process. As AI continues to evolve, so too will your knowledge base. Embrace the opportunity to learn and grow alongside this transformative technology. In the final section, we'll explore the importance of shaping the future of AI responsibly.

Shaping the Future of AI

The incredible potential of AI comes with a responsibility to ensure its development and use are ethical and beneficial to all. Here's why your voice matters in shaping the future of AI:

- Combating Bias: Artificial intelligence (AI) algorithms are capable of reproducing social biases if they are trained on data that reproduces these biases. We need different points of view in AI development to ensure justice and inclusion.
- Ensuring Transparency: Understanding how AI systems arrive at decisions is crucial. By advocating for transparency, we can build trust in AI and hold developers accountable for potential biases.

- Guiding AI for Good: AI has the potential to solve some of humanity's most pressing challenges: climate change, disease eradication, and resource scarcity. By actively engaging in discussions about AI's role in society, we can steer its development towards positive outcomes.

So how can you get involved? Here are a few ways to contribute to a responsible AI future:

- Stay Informed: Follow reputable sources that discuss AI developments and ethical considerations.
- Support Ethical AI Initiatives: Look for organizations advocating for responsible AI development and lend your voice to their causes.
- Engage in Open Discussions: Talk to friends, family, and colleagues about AI. Sharing your perspective and learning from others fosters a more informed and engaged citizenry.

The future of AI is not predetermined. It's a story we collectively write. By embracing AI's potential while advocating for responsible development, we can ensure AI becomes a powerful tool for progress, enriching our lives and building a brighter future for all.

Conclusion

Our exploration of AI has hopefully shed light on this transformative technology. We've moved from the realm of science fiction to a world where AI invisibly but undeniably shapes our daily lives. By overcoming misconceptions and embracing AI as a tool, we unlock a treasure trove of potential for personal and societal advancement.

The journey doesn't end here. As AI continues to evolve, so too will our understanding and interaction with it. Remember, the key is to approach AI with curiosity and a willingness to learn. Equip yourself with a foundational knowledge base, actively participate in shaping the responsible development of AI, and most importantly, embrace the potential of AI to empower you and the world around you. The future is bright, and with AI as our partner, we can achieve remarkable things.